WRITERS AND CRITICS

Chief Editors
A. NORMAN JEFFARES
R. L. C. LORIMER

Advisory Editors
DAVID DAICHES
C. P. SNOW

Kafka is undoubtedly one of the four or five first-rate European writers of this century. He stands at a central point in any discussion of the literature or civilisation of the Western world in contemporary times. Charles Osborne, in this study, describes him as both the "symptom and product of his age." This book provides the reader with an invaluable and highly readable introduction to Kafka's life and work. It traces, through his life, personal papers, short stories, and novels, the themes of guilt, isolation, and despair which Kafka relentlessly explored. Charles Osborne suggests a development towards self-knowledge in his final novel *The Castle*.

The author is well-known as poet, editor, and a critic both of literature and of music. An Australian, formerly Assistant Editor of the *London Magazine*, he is now Deputy Literature Director of the Arts Council of Great Britain

KAFKA

CHARLES OSBORNE

OLIVER AND BOYD
EDINBURGH AND LONDON

OLIVER AND BOYD LTD
Tweeddale Court
Edinburgh 1

39A Welbeck Street
London W.1

First published 1967

Printed in Great Britain for Oliver and Boyd Ltd
by Robert Cunningham and Sons Ltd, Alva

CONTENTS

To K.

"The distance to my fellow-man is for me a very long one."—from Kafka's Notebooks

"What could have enticed me into this desolate land but the desire to stay here?"—*The Castle*

ACKNOWLEDGMENTS

Acknowledgments are due to the following publishers for permission to quote from the works specified: to Secker and Warburg Ltd. for Kafka, *Wedding Preparations in the Country*, *In the Penal Settlement*, *America*, *The Trial* and *The Castle*; to Schocken Books Inc. for Kafka, *Dearest Father*, *The Penal Colony* and *Amerika*, also for Brod, *Franz Kafka: A Biography*; to Alfred Knopf Inc. for Kafka, *The Trial* and *The Castle*.

The photograph on the front cover is reproduced by permission of Archiv Klaus Wagenbach

ABBREVIATED TITLES USED IN
THE REFERENCES

BFK	=	Max Brod: *Biography of Franz Kafka.*
WP	=	Franz Kafka: *Wedding Preparations in the Country.*
LM	=	Franz Kafka: *Letters to Milena.*
DFK	=	*The Diaries of Franz Kafka.*
PS	=	Franz Kafka: *In the Penal Settlement.*
DS	=	Franz Kafka: *Description of a Struggle* and *The Great Wall of China.*
A	=	Franz Kafka: *America.*
Neider	=	Charles Neider: *Kafka, His Mind and Art.*
T	=	Franz Kafka: *The Trial.*
C	=	Franz Kafka: *The Castle.*

CHAPTER I

THE LIFE

Franz Kafka was born in Prague on 3 July 1883 into a family of Czechoslovakian Jews. His father, Hermann Kafka, was a merchant with a wholesale haberdashery warehouse. The family came from Wosseck in South Bohemia where Hermann's father had been a butcher. Hermann's youth had obviously been a hard one, but his enormous endurance and capacity for work enabled him to lift himself out of his lowly origins, maintain an important business, and bring up a family in typical middle-class style. Hermann's wife, Julie Löwy, came from rather different stock. Her family had been mildly raffish, producing eccentric scholars and dreamers.

Franz was the eldest child of Hermann and Julie. His two brothers died in infancy, but three more children, all girls, were born much later. Consequently, Kafka's childhood was a somewhat lonely one. After having had a series of governesses, he was sent to German schools where he was educated in German as a German, and it was only much later that he became conscious of himself as Czech or Jewish. His first school was an elementary school in the Fleischmarkt, Prague, after which he attended the German Grammar School in the Old Town Square: a school which Max Brod mentions as being "the most severe in Prague."[1] Even as a child, Kafka was weak and delicate, and disposed to be extremely serious. He read a great deal, and could never be persuaded to take any exercise. A studio photograph of him, aged

[1] *BFK*, p. 15.

about five or six, shows a small boy in a kind of sailor-suit, with short breeches and long black stockings. He is too shy to look directly at the camera; his eyes are large, their gaze nervous but steady, his mouth is small. In his right hand he holds a stick, in his left a large hat. On neither object is his grip at all secure. His dark hair is brushed forward almost down to his eyebrows, curling away slightly in the centre. His ears are large.

Although the difference in their ages was too great for him to play regularly with his sisters, he did apparently write plays for them to act on his parents' birthdays. Some of their titles were remembered in later life by his sisters: *The Equilibrist, The Photographs Speak.*

The young Kafka's relationship with his father was an extremely complex one. It will be discussed in detail in the chapter dealing with his *Letter to my father*, but a few lines here from the *Letter* will give some idea of their author's childhood:

I was a nervous child, but I was certainly sulky, too, as children are; it is also true that my mother spoiled me, but I can't believe that I was a particularly difficult child, I can't believe that a friendly word, taking me quietly by the hand, a friendly glance, would not have got me to do anything that was wanted. Now at bottom you are a kind and gentle man (what I am about to say doesn't contradict this; I am talking only of the appearance you presented to the child), but not every child has the patience and the courage to go on looking until it has found the good side. You can only handle a child in the way you were created yourself, with violence, noise and temper, and in this case moreover you thought this was the most suitable way, because you wanted to bring me up to be a strong, brave boy.[2]

At the age of eighteen, Franz was admitted to Prague

[2] *BFK*, pp. 20-21.

University. On leaving school he had at first taken up the study of chemistry, for an entire fortnight, after which he switched his attention to German; this lasted one term. Then he fixed on law, and thus began his study of a subject his dislike of which he never attempted to conceal. This, for him, curious choice of profession requires some comment. Kafka at the time was inclined to suggest that he had given in to his father's demands and allowed himself to be defeated:

> There was no real freedom of choice of profession for me, I knew: compared with the main point every-thing will be as indifferent to me as the subjects I took in my secondary school, and so the only thing is to find a profession which will give the widest scope for this indifference, without hurting my vanity too much. So the law as the obvious thing. Feeble oppositional attempts of my vanity, of senseless optimism, like my fourteen days study of chemistry, my half-year of reading German, served only to strengthen my funda-mental conviction.[3]

But it seems just as likely that, already fired, however vaguely, with the idea of achieving something in the realm of art, the actual business of earning a living appeared to him as something different, less important, something to be put out of mind until the latest possible moment. No immediate decision about a future career was involved in commencing to study law. One might be called to the bar, enter the civil service, act in an advisory capacity to some private firm. The important thing was to be a student for several more years and see how one's inner life sorted itself out.

It was at university that Kafka first met Max Brod, his friend for life and future biographer, who was his junior by one year. They met as members of a students' union which congregated at the Reading and Lecture

[3] *BFK*, p. 35.

Room for German Students, in Prague. The union had
its social side, of course, but Kafka and Brod concerned
themselves mostly with an almost independent subgroup
called the Section for Literature and Art, and it was
through the meetings of this group that Kafka's feeling
for and interest in literature began to assume a shape and
a direction. His approach to literature was through
philosophy, was, in fact, through having problems of his
own. His entire childhood had posed various problems
to him, problems to which family life and traditional
religion had not provided satisfactory answers. It was for
help in the business of living that, as one naturally does
in adolescence, the young Kafka first turned to literature.
With the aid of a dictionary and the remnants of his
secondary school Greek, he read Plato. With Max Brod
he began to read Flaubert in French. Flaubert and
Goethe were to be amongst his best-loved writers for the
rest of his life.

One day, Kafka mentioned to Brod that he had written
a short story for a competition in a Viennese newspaper.
The story did not win a place, and has not survived, but
shortly after, in 1909, Kafka read to Brod the first
chapter of a novel, *Preparations for a Wedding in the
Country*. Brod, who had by this time begun to have essays
published in newspapers and magazines, and whose
first book had already appeared, was immediately impressed and delighted by this chapter:

> I got the impression immediately that he was no
> ordinary talent speaking, but a genius. My efforts to
> bring Kafka's works before the public began from that
> moment—an endeavour that was stronger than
> myself, and which indeed I made no effort to fight
> against, because I considered it right and natural.[4]

Brod's first method of advancing his friend's literary
career was simple and direct. In an article he wrote for

[4] *BFK*, p. 51.

the Berlin weekly, *Die Gegenwart*, he mentioned several prominent authors such as Thomas Mann and Wedekind, and included amongst them the name of Franz Kafka who had not published a word. Some months later, however, prose works of Kafka did begin to appear in print, in the journal *Hyperion* edited by Franz Blei, and in the Prague daily newspaper, *Bohemia*. All of this was due to the efforts of Brod.

In 1906 Kafka obtained his Doctorate in Jurisprudence at the German University of Prague, and proceeded to work for the required period of one year in the courts: not that he intended for one moment to take up the law as a profession, but simply to give himself time to relax after the examinations, and time to consider again how he was really going to earn a living. A literary career was out of the question. Even if he had considered it possible to live by his writing, he would not have done so. The idea of turning his gift to practical advantage would have seemed abhorrent to him then. With his friend Brod he began to look for an office job, not in an ordinary commercial firm which would take up one's entire day, but in one of those more exclusive offices where one's hours were from eight till two, so that afternoons and evenings were kept free for reading, writing, walking, visits to the theatre and so on. Jobs of this kind were mainly to be found in Government offices; and, eventually, in July 1908, Kafka found the right position as a clerk with the Worker's Accident Insurance Institute for the Kingdom of Bohemia. He worked in a department which studied methods of preventing accidents in industry. He even wrote, in 1909, a detailed report on the subject. Indeed, so much of his energy went into his office work that he began to find any creative writing difficult. Office hours always look shorter on paper than they really are, and the depressing barrenness of the daily routine was hardly conducive to an energetic private life. For a time Kafka tried sleeping in the afternoon and writing at night, but exhaustion eventually set in. In a letter to Brod, at this time, he writes:

> If only you knew how much I have to do! In my four district headquarters—apart from all my other work —people fall, as if they were drunk, off scaffolds and into machines, all the planks tip up, there are land-slides everywhere, all the ladders slip, everything one puts up falls down and what one puts down one falls over oneself. All these young girls in china factories who incessantly hurl themselves downstairs with mountains of crockery give one a headache.[5]

The tone in that passage is one of comic desperation, but in his private diary he has no need to disguise his condition. Constrained to show an interest in his father's factory and even to work there in the afternoons, he writes:

> What agony the factory costs me. Why did I not protest when they made me promise to work there in the afternoons! Of course no one makes me do it by force, but my father does by reproaches and K. by silence and my guilty conscience. I know nothing about the factory, and this morning when I was being shown over the factory I stood around helpless and like a whipped schoolboy. I swear I shall never be able to get to the bottom of all the details of the workings of the factory.[6]

The tension mounted over several months until he was half-seriously contemplating suicide. He conveyed his state of mind in a letter to Brod who was sufficiently alarmed to write to Kafka's mother. She, poor woman, was most upset, and suggested that they should let Franz off the job of supervising the factory, but continue to pretend to his father that he was visiting it daily.

In his letters of this period, as well as in his diary

[5] *BFK*, p. 70.   [6] *BFK*, p. 72.

entries, one finds Kafka not only being bitter about the conditions under which he is forced to live, but also, amidst this distraction, attempting to formulate a philosophy to guide him. Again and again there recur phrases which make it clear that Kafka's idea of literature, even then, was that it was a specialised department of philosophy: a kind of creative philosophy. He wrote because he wanted answers to the problems that tormented him. Life was chaos, and he had to write some semblance of order into it. A lonely, unsociable man attempting to force himself into the community-life around him, somewhat in the manner of K.'s attempt to connect, to engage, in *The Castle*.

His summer holidays from the office were usually spent with Brod on long walking-tours, sunbathing and swimming. In 1909 they went to Riva. While they were there, they read in a local newspaper that the first flying meeting was about to take place at Brescia. Neither of the young men had yet seen a flying machine, and Brod recounts how very keen Kafka was to make the trip to see one. "How false the view is that considers Kafka was at home in an ivory tower, a world of phantasies, far removed from life, and imagines him as at ascetic consumed by nothing other than religious speculations. He was entirely different: he was interested in everything new, topical, technical, as for example, in the beginnings of the film; he never proudly withdrew himelf, even in the case of abuses and excrescences of modern development. . . ."[7]

At this time, Kafka had not written anything for several months, and by goading him into a competition to see which of the two would write the best account of the flying meeting, Brod succeeded in starting him off again. Kafka's article, "The Aeroplanes at Brescia," was published in September 1909 in *Bohemia*; a pleasant little essay with excellent descriptions of Blériot, Curtiss, and

[7]*BFK*, p. 82.

the other flyers, and thumb-nail sketches of some of the celebrities present. ("Over the railings of the stand peers the strong face of Puccini with a nose that one might well call a drinker's nose.")[8]

This was the first of many times, apparently, that Brod was to cajole, coax or threaten Kafka into writing. Brod claims in the *Biography* that it is thanks to him that Kafka's diary ever came into being, and this is probably true. In 1910 the friends took their holidays in Paris, but while there Franz developed a small carbuncle and, dissatisfied with the French doctors, went back home to Prague after a few days. In the same year, Brod introduced him to a Polish-Yiddish troupe of actors with whose world Kafka immediately became entranced. He wrote in his diary about the theatre, its actors and actresses and their private lives, and became a great friend of the young actor Isak Löwy. In fact, he began to write a pseudo-autobiography of Löwy, based on his talks with him, and also helped to arrange tours for the company to all the Zionist Clubs in Bohemia.

We are so used to the idea that Kafka's sex-life was in a state of chaotic repression, which it undoubtedly was in the latter part of his life, that we perhaps find it difficult to credit Brod's stories of the teen-age Franz often spending evenings in wine bars with pretty girls. According to Brod, at one time Kafka was infatuated with a barmaid called Hansi, of whom nevertheless he took a sufficiently detached view to be able to say wittily that whole cavalry regiments had ridden across her body. Yet even at this stage there are stumbling-blocks in the way of the most casual sex-relationship. A sad letter to Brod, written in 1908, states: ". . . I must go and look for someone who will only just give me a friendly pat so urgently that yesterday I went to a hotel with a whore. She is too old to feel melancholy any more; but she is sad, even though she doesn't wonder at it, that one is not

[8] *BFK*, pp. 176-7.

so loving with a whore as one is with a mistress. I didn't bring her any comfort, because she didn't bring me any."[9]

In 1912 Brod and Kafka travelled to Weimar. They had been studying Goethe together for years; indeed, Kafka spoke of him with great awe, and the journey to "his" town was made in a spirit of reverence. On the way they passed through Leipzig where Brod introduced Kafka to Ernst Rowohlt and Kurt Wolff who were running a publishing house. Brod was anxious for his friend to be published in book form, but Kafka's attitude to this was one of extreme ambivalence. The Leipzig publishers agreed, in principle, to publish him, and asked only that he collect together those of his writings that he wished to see published in a volume. Returning to Prague, Kafka began to assemble from the diaries, aphorisms and beginnings of stories, one complete manuscript. It was while he was engaged in this task that he decided everything he had written was worthless. Brod attempted to reason with him; nevertheless the material finally chosen made up a very short book indeed, and in 1913 *Betrachtung* (Meditation) appeared in print as ninety-nine pages of gigantic type.

It seemed that with the publication of his first book some further creative flow was released in Kafka: in the same year he completed a short story, *The Verdict*, set to work on his first novel, *America*, and broke off to write one of his finest stories, *The Metamorphosis*. The first chapter of *America* was published separately by Kurt Wolff in Leipzig.

In the summer of 1913 Kafka had met a girl from Berlin, Felice Bauer, and had fallen heavily in love with her. When she returned to Berlin, they corresponded. At first she appeared to reciprocate Kafka's affection, but she was of a practical nature and soon began to have doubts as to the suitability of Franz as a reliable husband.

[9] *BFK*, p. 93.

K B

They considered themselves engaged, but eventually Felice decided she wanted to break it off. Kafka, both in his letters to her and in his diaries, tormented himself and her with doubts and fears. He was frantic when he did not hear from her, he was beset with fears and scruples when he did hear. Typically, he drew up for himself a document listing the reasons for and against his marriage. It is significant that of the seven points he mentions, only one, the first, is *for* marriage: "Inability to bear living alone." All the others were strong reasons why he should stay single. These were his seven points:

1. Inability to bear living alone, not any inability to live, quite the contrary; it is even unlikely that I understand how to live together with someone; but to bear the onslaught of my own life, the onslaught of time and old age, the vague pressure of the itch to write, my sleeplessness, the near approach of madness—to bear all this alone I am unable. Perhaps I should fit in naturally. My connection with F. will lend my existence greater powers of resistance.

2. Everything immediately gives me to think. Every joke in the comic papers; every memory of Flaubert and Grillparzer; the sight of the nightshirts laid out on my parents' twin beds made for the night; Max's marriage. Yesterday N.N. said "All the married men (among our friends) are happy, I don't understand it"—when he said this, it also give me to think, and I became frightened again.

3. I must be alone a great deal. All that I have accomplished is the result of being alone.

4. Everything that is not connected with literature I hate; it bores me to carry on conversations (even when they are concerned with literature); it bores me to pay calls, the joys and sorrows of my relatives bore me to the very soul. Conversation takes the importance, the seriousness and the truth out of everything, I think.

5. Fear of being tied to anyone, of overflowing into another personality. Then I shall never be alone any more.

6. In front of my sisters, this was especially so in my earlier days, I was often a quite different person than with other people. I laid myself open, was fearless, strong, unexpected, carried away, as I otherwise am only when I am writing. If I could only be these things before all the world through the intermediation of my wife! But wouldn't it in that case be at the expense of my writing? Only not that! Not that!

7. Single, I might perhaps one day really give up my job. Married, it would never be possible.[10]

Nevertheless, he proposed to Felice. The official engagement lasted for only one week in 1914, but the affair dragged on for years. The Great War began, Kafka started several works simultaneously, including *The Trial* and *In the Penal Colony*. He met Felice again in Bodenbach in 1915, in Marienbad in 1916, and noted in his diary: "I think it is impossible we should ever become one, but don't dare to say it, either to her or, at the decisive moment, to myself."[11] He made another of his lists for and against marriage, but in a letter to Max Brod he wrote: "Now it is all different and all right. Our compact is, in brief: Get married shortly after the war is over; take two or three rooms in a Berlin suburb; leave each one only his economic worries; F. will go on working as before, and I, well, that I can't yet say."[12]

Back in Prague, he made the experiment of living away from his family and taking rooms elsewhere. It is possible in Prague today to see some of Kafka's occasional apartments. One of the most fascinating is the room in a house next door to the Tyn Church. The house must originally have been part of the church, because the window in Kafka's room is a window in the wall of the

[10] *BFK*, p. 112.   [11] *BFK*, p. 119.   [12] *BFK*, p. 120.

nave, and looks directly down into the faces of the faith-
ful at prayer. One can easily imagine the pale Kafka
hiding behind his curtain, and peering down into the
church.

The psychological and economic obstacles to his
marriage proved too much for him. He had got as far as
taking a flat, paying the conventional calls on relatives
with Felice, and making all the necessary plans. On
9 July 1917 the couple even paid a formal call on Max
Brod. "The sight of the two, both rather embarrassed,
above all Franz, wearing an unaccustomed high stiff
collar, had something moving in it, and at the same time
something horrible."[13] And then Franz, finding no other
way out, called upon the catastrophe. He began to cough
up blood, Brod, in his journal for 24 August 1917, notes:
"Steps taken in the matter of Kafka's illness. He insists it is
psychic, just like something to save him from marriage."[14]

Catarrh of the lungs was diagnosed. There was danger
of tuberculosis, marriage was out of the question. A year
or so later, Felice married someone else.

It was after the war, when Kafka was staying with his
sister and her family at a Baltic seaside resort, that he met
Dora Diamant who worked in the kitchen of the Berlin
Jewish People's Home. At the time of their meeting Dora
was no more than twenty. She came from a fairly well-
to-do Polish Jewish family, but had left home to find her
own way in the world.

Kafka was studying Hebrew and, as Dora was a
Hebrew scholar, their first conversations were linguistic
ones. His interest in her rapidly deepened, and it was not
long before he had decided to leave Prague forever, and
live with Dora in Berlin. To the surprise of all who knew
him, he actually achieved this. For the first time he
seemed at peace. Brod says: "At last I saw my friend in
good spirits; his bodily health had got worse, it is true.
Yet for the time it was not even dangerous."[15] Kafka had

[13] *BFK*, p. 124.   [14] *BFK*, p. 127.   [15] *BFK*, p. 154.

finally found the independence of his parents that he had always longed for. He was able to sleep soundly, for almost the first time. He was able to write.

But it was not to last. The post-war inflation in Berlin made life difficult, and the winter of 1923 was a particularly hard one. Kafka had a small pension, but it was rendered totally inadequate by the changing economic circumstances. He earned very little from the publication of his stories, and only at times of the direst need would he accept money or food parcels from his family in Prague. His health began rapidly to fail. As long as he could, Kafka continued to attend lectures on the Talmud at the Jewish High School for Science. But by March 1924 it was obvious that his situation was extremely serious. Max Brod warned an uncle of Kafka's, Robert Klopstock who was a doctor, and together they brought him back to Prague, Dora followed him. He became worse, and had to be moved to a sanatorium in the Vienna Woods. The doctors at the sanatorium diagnosed tuberculosis of the larynx, and sent him to the Vienna Clinic, His doctor uncle broke off his Berlin duties to look after Franz until his death.

Conditions in the clinic in Vienna were far from ideal, and at the end of April Dora and Dr Klopstock were able to have the patient transferred to a pleasant nursing home outside Vienna at Kierling, near Klosterneuberg. By this time Kafka was in great pain. One of the doctors advised Dora to take him home to Prague, as they could do nothing for him. His lungs and his larynx were in such a condition that all that could be done was to relieve the pain by administering morphine.

In these last weeks, unable to speak very much, Kafka communicated with his visitors by writing messages. On Monday, 2 June, he was able to correct proofs of his book of stories, *The Hunger Artist*. The following day, the pain was intense, and he kept asking for relief. He was given injections, and then said to Klopstock, "Kill me, or else you are a murderer."[16] And slowly he passed through sleep into death.

This brief account of the forty years of Kafka's life leans heavily for most of its facts on Max Brod's biography. Indeed, we are all indebted to Max Brod for having, in a sense, made Kafka available to us. So indebted that there may even be a danger of our seeing Kafka completely through the eyes of his biographer and friend. In addition to its factual information, Brod's biography consists in great part of the author's own interpretations of Kafka's works, his personality, his actions, his beliefs. Reading the biography one sometimes has the impression that Kafka was a character created by Max Brod. We have, perhaps, too unquestioningly accepted his estimate of Kafka.

In the biography there is a chapter called "Religious Development" which is worth studying carefully. It is here, in particular, that Brod puts forward his view of Kafka as a writer of a much more optimistic kind than an unbiassed reading of the novels would suggest. Brod is concerned, also, to underline and emphasise Kafka's religious tendencies, and even finds his violent scepticism useful when equating Kafka with Job:

Perhaps there have been men who have had a deeper, that is to say a less questioning faith than Kafka's —perhaps also there have been men with even more biting scepticism—that I don't know. But what I do know is the unique fact that in Kafka these two contradictory qualities blossomed out into a synthesis of the highest order. One might gather its importance into this sentence: Of all believers he was the freest from illusions, and among all those who see the world as it is, without illusions, he was the most unshakeable believer. It is the old question of Job.[17]

One must allow Brod his own temperament; but

[16] *BFK*, p. 165.   [17] *BFK*, p. 138.

psychology will be of greater help to us than religion in our understanding of Kafka. By considering each of the important works in turn in the following pages, we shall hope not to prove any theory, but simply to understand, using the evidence available, something of the nature and variety of this complex genius.

CHAPTER II

THE LETTERS AND DIARIES

Kafka's journals and letters provide us with evidence about the nature of his art. One of the most important documents is the *Letter to his Father*. It was written by Kafka in November 1919, but it was never actually delivered to his father. This *apologia pro sua vita* was brought into being by the tension that existed between father and son. It was begun, on one level, as an attempt to bridge the ever-widening gulf of misunderstanding between them, but on a deeper level it exists as Kafka's attempt to create himself in his own image. That painful crucial task which many creative artists of a certain temperament elect to face was for Kafka the cruellest necessity.

Kafka's father had, by his own efforts, made himself into a successful middle-class business-man. For him his own kind of life was the only good life, and it was impossible for him to understand how any son of his could fail to agree. From his early childhood on, the young Kafka sought the good opinion of his father, but not, as a really weak character might have done, by attempting to emulate his father's character and personality. He already recognised that it was diametrically opposed to his own and, by insisting on the difference in their natures, he sought to be accepted by his father as a person in his own right, and not simply as an extension of himself:

> I'm not going to say, of course, that I have become what I am only as a result of your influence. That

would be very much exaggerated (and I am indeed inclined to this exaggeration). It is indeed quite possible that even if I had grown up entirely free from your influence I still could not have become a person after your own heart. I should probably have still become a weakly, timid, hesitant, restless person, neither Robert Kafka nor Karl Hermann, but yet quite different from what I really am, and we might have got on with each other excellently. I should have been happy to have you as a friend, as a chief, an uncle, a grandfather, even indeed (though this rather more hesitantly) as a father-in-law. Only as what you are, a father, you have been too strong for me, particularly since my brothers died when they were small and my sisters only came along much later, so that I had to bear the whole brunt of it all alone, something I was too weak for.[1]

His father's world was completely inaccessible to Kafka. Not only was it inaccessible, it was also, he felt, a threat to his own security, to his own picture of himself. It is significant that at one point Kafka considered issuing his collected works under the title *The Attempt to Escape from Father*. His writing was the only means he had to escape the stifling and unreasoning domination of the father: the danger there was that the obsessive theme of the father might come to dominate his work. And, in a sense, it did. Kafka never really escaped his father. And understandably so: his father was necessary to Kafka's art, and in the final resort it is art that triumphs over life.

In the *Letter to his Father* Kafka lights on one of the sources of the terrifying nightmare quality of much of his later writing. He is referring to what he calls the "only one episode in the early years of which I have a direct memory."

[1] *WP*, p. 159.

You may remember it too. Once in the night I kept on whimpering for water, not, I am certain, because I was thirsty, but probably partly to be annoying, partly to amuse myself. After several vigorous threats had failed to have any effect, you took me out of bed, carried me out on to the *pavlatche* and left me there alone for a while in my nightshirt, outside the shut door. I am not going to say that this was wrong—perhaps at that time there was really no other way of getting peace and quiet that night—but I mention it as typical of your methods of bringing up a child and their effect on me. I daresay I was quite obedient afterwards at that period, but it did me inner harm. What was for me a matter of course, that senseless asking for water, and the extraordinary terror of being carried outside were two things that I, my nature being what it was, could never properly connect with each other. Even years afterwards I suffered from the tormenting fancy that the huge man, my father, the ultimate authority, would come almost for no reason at all and take me out of bed in the night and carry me out on to the *pavlatche*, and that therefore I was such a mere nothing for him.[2]

Here we see one of the beginnings of that sense of guilt which pervades Kafka's life and work. Invariably, in his later life, we find him explaining, justifying his actions, always rationally and sensibly, defending his behaviour against an accusing higher authority. Against father. Against God. Finally, against himself as well. For the penetrating accusations are made by the deeper part of his being. The reasonableness of the defendant at times breaks down. Far from answering the charges of his judge, he is dredging up far more terrifying accusations by a schizoid method of self-accusation.

The only area of feeling in which Kafka and his

[2] *WP*, pp. 161-2.

father were able to approach each other with some degree of freedom from their respective neuroses was that of Judaism. But even here their minds and temperaments met only on the most superficial level. For the father, Judaism was an acceptable way of life, it was his religion to which he paid a perfunctory kind of deference. Kafka's questing mind could not, of course, accept this as real or significant. As a youth, he found the technicalities of the Jewish faith of no interest to him. When he was older, and became deeply intrigued by Jewish philosophy and religion, his very earnestness separated him still further from the conventional attitude of his father:

I have received a certain retrospective confirmation of this view of your Judaism from your attitude in recent years, when it seemed to you that I was taking more interest in Jewish things. As you have a dislike in advance of every one of my activities and particularly of the nature of my interest, so you have had it here too. But in spite of this general attitude, one would really have expected that here you would make a little exception. It was, after all, Judaism of your Judaism that was here stirring and thus with it the possibility too of the start of new relations between us. I do not deny that if you had shown interest in them these things might, for that very reason, have become suspect in my eyes. For I do not dream of asserting that I am in this respect in any way better than you. But it never came to putting it to the test. Through my meditation Judaism became abhorrent to you and Jewish writings unreadable; they "nauseated" you. This may have meant that you were insisting that only that Judaism which you had shown me in my childhood was the right one, and beyond that there was nothing.[3]

[3] *WP*, p. 196.

The ambivalence of the relationship between Kafka
and his father, or rather (since it was so one-sided an
affair) of the relationship of Kafka to his father, pervades
most of his writing. It does not require much psychological acumen to perceive that the nature of this
personal experience determined the nature of Kafka's
religious experience, and that Kafka's love of and distrust of God, his desire to bring punishment down on his
head from the Almighty to enable him to atone and lift
the burden of irrational guilt that lay heavily on his
shoulders, stems directly from his father complex. The
explanation, as far as it goes, is an obvious one; but,
though it shows us something of the primary cause of the
aesthetic experience, it cannot enlighten us as to its
nature. Similarly, in the *Letter to his Father*, we find much
in the father's attitude that shows clearly the future total
misunderstanding being brought into existence step by
step:

> You put special trust in bringing children up by
> means of irony, and this was most in keeping with your
> superiority over me. An admonition from you generally
> took this form: "Can't you do it in such-and-such a
> way? That's too hard for you, I suppose. You haven't
> the time, of course?" and so on. And each such ques-
> tion would be accompanied by malicious laughter and
> a malicious face. One was so to speak already punished
> before one even knew that one had done something
> bad.[4]

Irony opposes: it is love that penetrates. And slowly,
over the childhood years, the opposing wall was constructed between father and son. Eventually Kafka
reached a stage where it was no longer possible for him
to attempt intellectually to understand his father. The
frightening weight of authority on one side of the wall,
and of guilt on the other, pushed against each other.

[4] *WP*, p. 172.

Finally Kafka is ready to judge himself guilty on all counts; most of all, perhaps, guilty of the crime of being innocent.

In this *Letter to his Father* which his father never saw, Kafka was talking to himself. In the *Letters to Milena* he is desperately concerned with communicating his deepest feelings to another human being. Milena was the translator of some of Kafka's stories into Czech. She came of a very old Prague family, and was a remarkable woman on many counts, not simply because Kafka loved her. The world she moved in, that of Viennese literary life in the years immediately following 1918, was not one to which she was well fitted by temperament. Her Dostoevskian restlessness of character was on too large a scale. When she and Kafka met, Milena was a married woman and Kafka was already involved with Dora. Their passionate attachment could hardly have had a very happy outcome, and indeed it began to disintegrate after barely a year. The letters to which it gave rise, however, are not only intensely moving in themselves, but also unusual in that through them we catch a glimpse of an extension of Kafka's personality that we do not get in his fiction, or even in the diaries: a temporarily untense, relaxed, gentle human being, forgetful for a while of the furies that pursued him. Admittedly, we receive this picture only at the beginning of the correspondence:

> I live here pretty well, more care the mortal body could hardly stand, the balcony of my room is lowered into a garden, surrounded, overgrown by flowering shrubs (the vegetation here is strange, in a weather which in Prague practically freezes the puddles, the flowers open slowly in front of my balcony) at the same time fully exposed to the sun (or rather to the deeply clouded sky, as it has been for nearly a week) lizards and birds, ill-assorted couples, visit me.[5]

[5] *LM*, p. 21.

As the relationship develops, Kafka's inexorable self-destructive or self-punishing impulses reassert themselves, and the letters become more like some of the feverish journal entries:

> The reason I ask whether you won't be afraid is that the person of whom you write doesn't exist and never existed, the one in Vienna didn't exist, nor did the one in Gmünd, though the latter one more so and he shall be cursed. To know this is important for, should we get together, the Viennese or even the one from Gmünd will reappear, in all innocence, as though nothing had happened, whereas below, the real one— unknown to all and himself, existing even less than the others (why doesn't he finally come up and show himself?)—will raise his threatening hand and smash everything once again.[6]

When Milena mentions she has had 'flu. Kafka's typical method of relating this information to his own condition leads him to write:

> So you've had the flu. Well, at least I can't reproach myself for having had an especially gay time here (sometimes I don't understand how human beings have discovered the notion of "gaiety," probably it has just been computed as a contrast to sadness).[7]

The life they at one time thought they might have together turned out not to be possible. The letters become less frequent, more formal. "No, Milena," writes Kafka at the beginning of this sad last phase, "the possibility of a shared life which we thought we had in Vienna, does not exist, under no condition, it didn't even exist then. I had looked 'over my fence,' had just held on to the top with my hands, then I fell back again with lacerated hands."[8]

The last letters reveal an increasing urgency in the ever

[6] *LM*, p. 205.   [7] *LM*, p. 209.   [8] *LM*, pp. 214-15.

more frequent passages of self-awareness, self-conscious-ness, self-analysis. It is as though Kafka, knowing that his time was limited, were concerned with stating his nature as clearly as possible. These passages move through neurasthenic illness ("not one calm second is granted me, nothing is granted me . . . I can't carry the world on my shoulders, can barely stand my winter overcoat on them")[9] to a rare, pure, sad acceptance of his tortured condition:

It's more or less as though someone, each time before taking a walk, had not only to wash and comb himself and so on—this alone is tiresome enough—but he also (since, each time, he lacks the necessary for the walk) has to sew his clothes as well, make his shoes, manu-facture his hat, whittle his walking stick, and so on. Of course he's not able to do all this very well, perhaps they hold together for the length of a few streets, but when he reaches the Graben, for instance, they suddenly all fall apart and he stands there naked among rags and tatters. And now the torture of running back to the Altstädter Ring! And in the end he probably runs into a mob engaged in Jew-baiting in the Eisen-gasse.

Don't misunderstand me, Milena, I'm not saying that this man is lost, not at all, but he is lost if he goes to the Graben, where he disgraces himself and the world.[10]

Kafka's Diaries, covering the years between 1910 and 1923, are published as edited by Max Brod. In a post-script to the second of the two volumes, Dr Brod writes:

The text of the two volumes of the Diaries is as com-plete as it was possible to make it. A few passages, apparently meaningless because of their fragmentary nature, are omitted. In most instances no more than a

---

[9] *LM*, p. 219.   [10] *LM*, pp. 219-20.

few words are involved. In several (rare) cases I omitted things that were too intimate, as well as scathing criticism of various people that Kafka certainly never intended for the public.[11]

It is to be hoped that a fuller text will become available in the course of time. One wonders what kind of detail, libel apart, Dr Brod considered too intimate. The jottings, phrases, the beginnings of stories, incidents from daily life reported raw, dreams. Often, one of the published stories will be found in adumbration in the Diaries. This was the battlefield: it was here that Kafka continually wrestled with the problems that beset him. Problems of style, of technique, of expression and, behind them, the larger problem of how to live in the world, how to find the way to his own true nature. To force a way through the complexity to the inner purity that Kafka never doubted was there. Here in the Diaries are the heights of joy attained by the creative artist and the depths of despair plumbed by the suffering man. One of the earliest entries, that for 16 December 1910, begins: "I won't give up the diary again. I must hold on here, it is the only place I can."[12] It then breaks off, as do so many of the entries, to become notes on what he was reading at the time, notes which indicate, however, how closely and seriously he read:

Hebbel praises Justinus Kerner's *Reiseschatten*. "And a book like this hardly exists, no one knows it."

Die Strasse der Verlassenheit by W. Fred. How do such books get written? A man who on a small scale produces something fairly good here blows up his talent to the size of a novel in so pitiful a manner that one becomes ill even if one does not forget to admire the energy with which he misuses his own talent.[13]

[11] *DFK*, Vol. 2, p. 327.   [12] *DFK*, Vol. 1, p. 33.
[13] *DFK*, Vol. 1, p. 34.

The following day he is bewailing the fact that he has destroyed almost all that he has written in the previous year. There are jottings in these pages which could have come from the journals of almost any other twentieth-century writer, Gide, Scott Fitzgerald, Camus, passages which express the increasingly paralysing self-consciousness of our century. The terrifying inability to act, to perform even the simplest function such as packing a suitcase, posting a letter, that can occasionally overcome the healthiest and most extravert of temperaments, this was something that Kafka lived with throughout his entire life. Holding his head high enough not to drown was his preoccupation and a constant necessity. And this in a sea in which, to him, there appeared to be no other bathers. He was alone. It is not surprising that there were no other bathers: the sea was his own personality, in which he was almost completely submerged. The torture is from within, whence should also come the surge to escape. This the guilt-ridden Kafka lacked. He did not seek freedom, he sought merely the technical means to observe and record his punishment and despair. Where-ever he looked he saw himself, and this was at once his limitation and the finest definition of his strength:

January 12. I haven't written down a great deal about myself during these days, partly because of laziness (I now sleep so much and so soundly during the day, I have greater weight while I sleep), but also partly because of the fear of betraying my self-perception. This fear is justified, for one should permit a self-perception to be established definitively in writing only when it can be done with the greatest completeness, with all the incidental consequences, as well as with entire truthfulness. For if this does not happen—and in any event I am not capable of it—then what is written down will, in accordance with its own purpose and with the superior power of the established, replace what has been felt only vaguely in such a way that the real feeling will disappear while the worthlessness of what has been noted down will be recognised too late.[14]

It is, in a way, extremely misleading to approach Kafka through the Diaries: misleading, indeed, to approach the work of almost any creative artist through his uncreative writings, but particularly in the case of the obsessive pessimist. One will usually get, from the Diaries, only the facts of pessimism. But the act of creation, however bleak the world created, is in itself a negation of pessimism. One must see before one can create, and it is in the Diaries that we find Kafka training himself, forcing himself, against the weight of his temperament, his personality and his family history, to see. To see, first, himself, "Today," he writes on 22 December 1910, "I do not even dare to reproach myself. Shouted into this empty day, it would have a disgusting echo."[15] This, it might seem, is seeing oneself with a sentimental self-pity, the sign of a weak mind. Kafka's mind, however, was anything but weak. It was a first-rate mind, tough and resilient. Why then, one wonders, did he not make stronger attempts to exorcise his devils, why did he hide from them in fear rather than fight to destroy them? It would be easy to see something pro-phetic in this, to see Kafka as a forerunner of the millions who in our time have lost the taste for, the urge towards, liberty. It was not Kafka, the man, who deeply and truly welcomed his fetters, it was his art which welcomed, which needed them. And Kafka was always ruled by his art, by the creative impulse. It cannot be said too often that the world in which Kafka's prose exists is an aesthetic world, not a neurasthenic one. Too frequently we look at a result as though we were examin-ing a symptom. Symptoms abound, admittedly, in the Diaries, but the novels, the completed stories, are works

[14] *DFK*, Vol. 1, p. 41.   [15] *DFK*, Vol. 1, p. 37.

of art. One can sometimes even follow, in the Diaries, the stages of metamorphosis. This, for instance, is the kind of entry that is pegged closely down to Kafka's self, indicative of little more than his day-to-day concern with himself:

> January 19. Every day, since I seem to be completely finished—during the last year I did not wake up for more than five minutes at a time—I shall either have to wish myself off the earth or else, without my being able to see even the most moderate hope in it, I shall have to start afresh like a baby.[16]

At about this time, Kafka was attending lectures on Theosophy by Dr Rudolf Steiner. He decided to visit the lecturer, and under the heading "My Visit to Dr Steiner" an account of their meeting appears in the 1911 Diary. Already, though presumably he wrote only a few hours after the events he describes, the measured tread of the artist supplants the hurried footsteps of the journalist. "My Visit to Dr Steiner" is halfway to being a Kafka story. The masterly scene-setting of the first paragraph, the semi-transformation of Kafka himself into K. in the second paragraph, these are indications difficult to ignore:

> A woman is already waiting (upstairs on the third floor of the Victoria Hotel on Jungmannstrasse), but urges me to go in before her. We wait. The secretary arrives and gives us hope. I catch a glimpse of him down the hall. Immediately thereafter he comes towards us with arms half spread. The woman explains that I was there first. So I walk behind him as he leads me into his room. His black Prince Albert which on those evenings when he lectures looks polished (not polished but just shining because of its clean

blackness) is now in the light of day (3 pm) dusty and even spotted, especially on the back and elbows.

In his room I try to show my humility, which I cannot feel, by seeking out a ridiculous place for my hat, I lay it down on a small wooden stand for lacing boots. Table in the middle, I sit facing the window, he on the left side of the table. On the table papers with a few drawings which recall those of the lectures dealing with occult physiology. An issue of the *Annalen für Naturphilosophie* topped a small pile of the books which seemed to be lying about in other places as well. However, you cannot look around because he keeps trying to hold you with his glance. But if for a moment he does not, then you must watch for the return of his glance. He begins with a few disconnected sentences: So you are Dr Kafka? Have you been interested in theosophy long?[17]

And then, every so often, usually preceded by several slightly differing earlier drafts, there emerges a short story, or an anecdote, or a paragraph from an unwritten tale:

"Will you stay here for a long time?" I asked. At my sudden utterance some saliva flew from my mouth as an evil omen.

"Does it disturb you? If it disturbs you or perhaps keeps you from going up, I will go away at once, but otherwise I should still like to remain, because I'm tired."[18]

Many of the diary entries, particularly in the earlier years, are accounts of the Jewish actors whose company Kafka frequented. Often he simply describes the various plays and performances, or the way a certain actress walks, her beauty, her intelligence. Occasionally, a poetic and chilling insight is scrawled onto the page:

[17] *DFK*, Vol. 1, pp. 57-58.　　　　[18] *DFK*, Vol. 1, p. 45.

Sometimes it seems that the play is resting up in the flies, the actors have drawn down strips of it the ends of which they hold in their hands or have wound about their bodies for the play, and that only now and then a strip that is difficult to release carries an actor, to the terror of the audience, up in the air.[19]

Always the sense of strain, of toil, the persistent attempt to write, to force words up and out and onto the page. "When I begin to write after a rather long interval," he says, "I draw the words as if out of the empty air. If I capture one, then I have just this one alone and all the toil must begin anew."[20]

It is the creative artist, not the tired being almost paralysed into immobility by his neuroses, who wrote the memorable entry for 21 July 1912:

Don't despair, not even over the fact that you don't despair. Just when everything seems over with, new forces come marching up, and precisely that means that you are alive. And if they don't, then everything is over with here, once for all.[21]

This is the closest, however, that Kafka comes to railing against fate, the nearest he gets to rebelling against "what must be." It is a kind of religious faith that keeps him from despair, the same faith that leads him to speak of writing as a form of prayer. But it is a passive quasi-Christian kind of faith. There is nothing of Prometheus in Kafka. He is far readier to suffer than to defy. There is a sense in which his refusal, or his inability, to fight meant that he therefore did not even escape from himself, from a final and complete absorption in himself. Totally concerned with his own suffering, his glance turned always deeper within himself. What he saw, he saw with remarkable insight, but what he saw was

---

[19] *DFK*, Vol. 1, p. 119.   [20] *DFK*, Vol. 1, p. 177.
[21] *DFK*, Vol. 1, pp. 290-1.

himself. The world, for Kafka, was really himself and his
guilt. Since he was almost nothing but genius, his world
was built of the constant confrontation of genius with
guilt, reflected in the various masochistic fantasies of the
Diaries:

> To be pulled in through the ground-floor window of
> a house by a rope tied around one's neck and to be
> yanked up, bloody and ragged, through all the ceilings,
> furniture, walls and attics, without consideration, as if
> by a person who is paying no attention, until the
> empty noose, dropping the last fragments of me when
> it breaks through the roof tiles, is seen on the roof.[22]

To enable himself to concentrate exclusively upon
his own guilt, he determines to shut himself off from
everyone to the point of insensibility. "Make an enemy
of everyone," he advises himself, "speak to no one."[23]
There are times, however, when he yearns for spiritual,
mental and physical health, only immediately to distrust
its effect upon him. On 6 November 1913 he writes:

> Whence the sudden confidence? If it would only
> remain! If I could go in and out of every door in this
> way, a passably erect person. Only I don't know
> whether I want that.[24]

Throughout all this, there are the constant attempts to
write stories, to begin novels. "Again tried to write,
virtually useless"[25] one reads. Or "The old incapacity.
Hardly ten days interrupted in my writing, and already
cast aside."[26] Or "Wrote little today and yesterday. Dog
story."[27] Or, more often, entries like this one of 23 March
1915: "Incapable of writing a line."[28] Attempting analysis
of his incapability, and of his various nervous disorders,

---

[22] DFK, Vol. I, p. 291.   [23] DFK, Vol. I, p. 297.
[24] DFK, Vol. I, p. 307.   [25] DFK, Vol. II, p. 113.
[26] DFK, Vol. II, pp. 113-14.   [27] DFK, Vol. II, p. 114.
[28] DFK, Vol. II, p. 119.

he finds that noise no longer disturbs him. After all, the deeper one digs into oneself, the quieter it becomes.

It is this continual settling of accounts with himself, coming to terms with his condition that one finds most fascinating and moving in the Diaries. Indeed, it is impossible not to be touched by the sheer clarity, and therefore terror, of Kafka's self-knowledge as revealed in the Diaries. But, unlike, say, another famous diarist, André Gide, Kafka was not a man of letters. He was not consciously using the journal form as a vehicle for his thoughts on literature and life. Gide's Journals can, perhaps, be fairly said to be his finest contribution to literature, Kafka's, though inextricably bound up with his purely creative *œuvre*, are finally merely incidental to it. The Diaries are flung up, like hastily-shovelled earth, as Kafka feverishly digs deeper, in his compulsive act of self-discovery through excavation. The deeper burrow-ings produced the great works of fiction. When genius is finally face to face with silence and guilt, the world, friends, sexual anxiety, and all other extraneousness left behind, the creative equation is made. Genius plus guilt equals creation. It is to the fruits of Kafka's exclusively creative activity that we must now direct our attention, remembering, of course, their background, while con-sidering them not as extensions of their author's neurosis, but from the purely aesthetic viewpoint from which they demand to be seen. It is important, having considered Kafka the man through the facts of his life and the fantasies of his Diaries, not to allow one's picture of him to prejudice one's attitude to the novels and stories. The impulse to consider all his writings simply as the records he has left of his prosecutions, indeed persecutions, of himself, is itself a neurotic urge and is to be resisted. Too much Kafka criticism, by following this line, has done a great disservice to one of the most outstanding stylists in the German language.

CHAPTER III

THE SHORTER FICTION

The earliest work of Kafka's of any stature that has been preserved is *Description of a Struggle* (*Beschreibung eines Kampfes*) which he wrote at the age of nineteen or twenty. As its appearance in the English Definitive Edition is spread over two volumes in a rather confusing manner, a word or two of clarification is necessary. The volume entitled *In the Penal Settlement* opens with what are called "Two Dialogues from a work later destroyed: Description of a Struggle." But in fact the completed work was not destroyed, and can be read almost entire in the later volume called *Description of a Struggle* and *The Great Wall of China* (in a translation by James and Tania Stern that considerably improves upon the earlier and stiffer version of the Dialogues by Edwin and Willa Muir.) So the "Two Dialogues" on their own can be ignored. However, in Kafka's manuscript, after the Fat Man episode there is a section called "Children on a Country Road." This will be found, printed as the first of a series of pieces under the title "Meditation," in *In the Penal Settlement*.

It must be said that Kafka himself connived at the separate publication of episodes of *Description of a Struggle*, and, indeed, of other works. But since his intentions regarding the structure and composition of the piece are perfectly clear, it seems pointless now not to read the story as it was originally conceived. Max Brod, however, to whom we must be grateful for preserving the manuscript and eventually rediscovering it in his library in 1935, writes in detail in a Postscript to the German edition of his sound reasons for printing the work in the form in which it has been translated.

If one insists on the correct dovetailing of these fragmentary episodes into one another, it is because Kafka's sense of form in this, one of his earliest completed works, is already functioning superbly. He is so often thought of as having no architectonic sense at all, of never giving a thought to the shape of his fantasies, that it is instructive, and surely of some significance, to note that the chinese-box-like structure of *Description of a Struggle* is most consciously and carefully planned.

In its first section, the narrator describes the last moments of a party at a house in Prague. He is approached by a fellow guest, and they leave the house together. They walk through the deserted streets of the city, and they talk. Their conversation is wild and unrealistic, but the description of the streets, squares, and quays through which they walk is, on the contrary, most realistic. It is possible in Prague today to wander the same streets, to see the same buildings, churches, and monuments. His nightmarish frenzy is set in a very real and familiar landscape. Even the names of the Mühlenturm, the Karlsbrücke, the Seminarkirche seem to anchor the reader down and force him to consider the symbolism of the walkers' words and actions as they discuss themselves and their condition. "Discuss" is hardly the word, for their final indifference to each other's plight is strongly conveyed. As the section ends, the two of them are proposing to walk up to the top of the Laurenziberg.

Section Two is subtitled "Diversions or Proof That It's Impossible to Live," and is a curious interior monologue. The fellow-traveller has dissolved, and the narrator wanders in his own world of fantasy. This section is divided into four episodes, the third of which, "The Fat Man" is itself subdivided into four. After this section, there should follow the "Children on the Country Road," a strange, calm dream-like episode, before Section Three in which we return to the ostensible outer world of the narrator and his acquaintance who are now walking high up on the Laurenziberg.

The temptation to wrest a meaning from this uneven yet compelling work gradually lessens as one reads one's way through it and succumbs somewhat to its atmosphere or, one could almost say, its poetry. Nevertheless it is a restless, striving tale, and it is a tale about unrest, about the struggle to remain still, calm, and at peace with one-self and one's nature. A certain amount of incidental word-play is meaningless, is simply the young Kafka glorying, as he all too rarely did, in the pure sounds of words, phrases, sentences; but the work's real purpose is to dredge up into the air a kind of blue-print for existence. Is love the guide? Or dependence? Or stability? How can one become stable? On whom can one depend? With whom can one experience love? The acquaintance is fleeing from love, the narrator basks in the stability of his engagement to be married. But what remains longest in the reader's mind (and in the nar-rator's?) is the dream-picture, cruelly yet tenderly inserted into the moonlight world of the tale: the happy child in the country, innocent of all but the moment.

I heard the waggons rumbling past the garden fence, sometimes I even saw them through gently swaying gaps in the foliage. How the wood of their spokes and shafts creaked in the summer heat! Labourers were coming from the fields and laughing so that it was a scandal.

I was sitting on our little swing, just resting among the trees in my parents' garden.

On the other side of the fence the traffic never stopped. Children's running feet were past in a moment; harvest waggons with men and women perched on and around sheaves darkened the flowerbeds; towards evening I saw a gentleman slowly promenading with a walking-stick, and a couple of girls who met him arm-in-arm stepped aside into the grass as they greeted him.[1]

In its violent and strategic juxtaposition to the other sections of the story, this is in no danger of being considered weak or sentimental. Kafka's cunningly dramatic use of contrasting worlds and moods here approximates to the condition of music.

The Judgment (*Das Urteil*) is a much briefer and more compact story. Already the spontaneous improvisatory quality of earlier fragments and of *Description of a Struggle* is beginning to give way to a different kind of approach, or rather to a more emphatic, urgent style. Kafka usually wrote under stress and in short bursts, yet this story spilled from him overnight in one outbreak of energy. The element of fantasy in *The Judgment* is no less strong than in the earlier work we have been discussing, but it is quite differently used and is kept under a tighter control. Or, perhaps, what appears in the story to be fantasy is really what one might see by peering at reality through an X-ray machine. *The Judgment* admits quite easily of a theological interpretation or of a psychological one. Its meaning in theological terms lies so near the surface that we may fairly assume it to have been not too far below the consciousness of the author as he wrote it. Its psychological meaning, however, is unmistakably there, giving it validity and depth.

The tale concerns a young merchant, George Bendemann. Since his mother's death, his father has been losing interest in, and therefore control over, the family business, responsibility for which has passed in large part into George's hands. When the story begins, George has just finished writing a letter to an old friend of his who

[1] *PS*, p. 19.

has been living in Russia for some years. His business in St Petersburg, once flourishing, has been going downhill for sometime. George hesitates to write advising him to come home and start again, for he is too sensitive to thrust his own business success in his friend's face. And this same helpless consideration for his friend's feelings is the reason he has put off mentioning he is engaged to be married. However, with the letter he has just written he has plucked up courage to break the news to his friend, and he goes into his father's room which he has not entered for months to tell him that he has done so. He is surprised to find the room so dark on such a sunny morning, and his father sitting in a corner surrounded by mementoes of his dead wife. He tells of what he has written, and his father becomes strangely interested in the St Petersburg friend. Then he accuses George of having invented the friend. He seems unwell and weak, so George carries him to bed, but the old man recovers sufficiently to launch into a terrifying denunciation of his son, this time alleging that George has neglected his friend in St Petersburg whom the old man has been corresponding with regularly and who has replaced George in his affections. His mad tirade rises to a climax in which he finally shouts "So now you know what else there is in the world besides yourself. Till now you've known only about yourself! An innocent child, yes, that you were, truly, but still more truly have you been a devilish human being! And therefore take note: I sentence you now to death by drowning!"[2] At these words, George feels himself impelled from the room. He rushes downstairs and out of the house, knocking aside his charwoman as he goes, races across the road and over the railings into the river.

George is destroyed, not by his father's mad judgment, but by his friend in St Petersburg or, to be more exact, by the inadequacy of his relationship with his friend in

[2] *PS*, p. 58.

St Petersburg. Or, in other words, by the inadequacy of the relationship between his conscious self and his unconscious. George's inner condition is beyond the possibility of healing or recovery. His self-confident success is meaningless. His refusal to face himself in the mirror of reality, symbolised by his keeping his friend at a great distance in a foreign country, destroys him. His father, whom we see only through George's extremely subjective vision, destroys him only in that he completely understands him. And George destroys himself, too, when, too late, self-knowledge is forced upon him. The struggle, whether between father and son or between Ego and Id is, as always with Kafka, the struggle between the devitalised, aimless existence, devoid of conscience or of free-will, and the harder, almost impossible road where each step forward is painful, whose end may be insanity, nothingness or creation, but whose way is at any rate the way of responsibility and awareness. At the moment of crisis, George fails. His flinging himself into the river was the final act of irresponsibility, though perhaps one should blame God, the father. Certainly if one inclines to see the father as God and the dead mother as the diminished power of the church or synagogue, the man is alone, self-confidently alone in his decisions until pulled up short by the necessarily irrational behaviour of God. Thus God destroys man.

Kafka's handling of the surface realism of his story becomes surer in *The Judgment*, covering completely, where it is meant to, the nervous disturbance that underlines the narrative throughout. The description of George's care of his father when the old man appears to be feeble engages one completely, distracts attention momentarily from the gathering storm:

Meanwhile George had succeeded in lowering his father down again and carefully taking off the woollen drawers he wore over his linen underpants and his socks. The not particularly clean appearance of this underwear made him reproach himself for having been neglectful. It should have certainly been his duty to see that his father had clean changes of underwear. He had not yet explicitly discussed with his bride-to-be what arrangements should be made for his father in the future, for they had both of them silently taken it for granted that the old man would go on living alone in the old house. But now he made a quick, firm decision to take him into his own future establishment. It almost looked, on closer inspection, as if the care he meant to lavish there on his father might come too late.[3]

Die Verwandlung has appeared in English translation both as "The Metamorphosis" and "The Transformation." Though it is better known under the former title, the latter is the one used in the Definitive Edition. This terrifying and pitiful comedy is a parable with an extraordinary emotive force. Its plot can be summarised briefly: George Samsa, a commercial traveller who lives in an apartment with his parents and sister, awakens one morning to find that he has been transformed into a gigantic cockroach. He still has his human consciousness, but is unable to make this clear to his family who, after their initial panic, are terribly ashamed of him and keep him locked in his room. As Gregor is obviously unable to continue working, the old father has to go to work as a bank messenger. The family takes in lodgers to help make ends meet. One evening the sister is playing the violin to the lodgers when Gregor, attracted by the sound of music, ventures out of his room. The lodgers, catching sight of him, are appalled. He is driven back into his room where, after a night of sleepless dejection, he dies.

It is hardly possible to overestimate the effect of this

[3] *PS*, p. 54.

long story, one of Kafka's most closely-knit and brilliantly calculated creations. The manner in which the several realistic sections of development are made to arise naturally and inevitably out of the central premise which is one of fantasy or nightmare, is particularly remarkable. Throughout the story Kafka touches a nerve-string of the human condition and plays upon it with incredible exactness. The finished work has almost the aspect of an anonymous urban folk-tale, so mysteriously does it appear to follow some hidden but irrefutable law of creation. The air of anonymity or, more exactly, objectivity is heightened by Kafka's prose style which here takes on an almost legal dryness, refusing the solaces of easy sentimentality in its terse pointedness. Feeling is conveyed directly through factual observation. The opening paragraph presents us immediately with the fantastic transformation:

> As Gregor Samsa awoke one morning from uneasy dreams he found himself transformed in his bed into a gigantic insect. He was lying on his hard, as it were armour-plated, back and when he lifted his head a little he could see his dome-like brown belly divided into stiff arched segments on top of which the bed-quilt could hardly keep in position and was about to slide off completely. His numerous legs, which were pitifully thin compared to the rest of his bulk waved helplessly before his eyes.[4]

After this, the story's development follows strictly logical lines. The reaction of the family, the feelings of Gregor Samsa himself, are all that one would expect once one admits, not the possibility of such a transformation, but the simple fact that it has happened. Every morning when one awakes one recreates the world. What if, however, one were to awaken to find that one had been recreated by the world, in the shape of a giant cock-

[4] *PS*, p. 63.

roach? What if, instead of the frightening disorientation of the moments of awakening, there is a permanent dislocation? Kafka's simple miracle in this story touches us somewhere very deeply and disturbingly. It is a nightmare with the consoling blanket of sleep swept aside.

The parable itself admits of various interpretations. It matters little to which of them one subscribes, as long as one does not lose sight of the story itself. The work of art, after all, is greater than the sum of its possible meanings, and this is deeply true of "The Metamorphosis." Its poetic and tragic detail is not to be ignored in the search for over-all meaning. In his inability to join hands joyfully with the world and his consequent transformation in the eyes of that world into something strange and non-human, Gregor resembles the figure of the artist. In his piteous attempts not to completely lose contact with his family and his employers (his audience?) he strengthens the resemblance. Kafka sees these moments almost as pure comedy:

"Mother, Mother," said Gregor in a low voice and looked up at her. The chief clerk, for the moment, had quite slipped from his mind; instead, he could not resist snapping his jaws together at the sight of the creaming coffee. That made his mother scream again, she fled from the table and fell into the arms of his father, who hastened to catch her. But Gregor had now no time to spare for his parents; the chief clerk was already on the stairs; with his chin on the banisters he was taking one last backward look. Gregor made a spring, to be as sure as possible of overtaking him; the chief clerk must have divined his intention, for he leapt down several steps and vanished; he was still yelling "Ugh!" and it echoed through the whole staircase.[5]

And then, without either the pace or the style of the

[5] *PS*, p. 81-82.

narrative being altered at this point, the comedy assumes a Chaplinesque pathos with the very next sentence:

Unfortunately, the flight of the chief clerk seemed completely to upset Gregor's father, who had remained relatively calm until now, for instead of running after the man himself, or at least not hindering Gregor in his pursuit, he seized in his right hand the walking-stick which the chief clerk had left behind on a chair, together with a hat and greatcoat, snatched in his left hand a large newspaper from the table and began stamping his feet and flourishing the stick and the newspaper to drive Gregor back into his room.[6]

And this ambivalence of mood, or rather sudden alternation of mood, is maintained throughout the story. Gregor dies because he is not sufficiently human, or because he is not sufficiently loved. It is the same thing.

Fantasy and fact were interchangeable to Kafka, and forty years after his death they are increasingly difficult to distinguish in the visible world. In 1920 one might have been able to call *In der Strafcolonie* (*In the Penal Settlement*) a sadistic nightmare. But now, after Hitler's Germany, Stalin's Russia, de Gaulle's Algeria, and Verwoerd's South Africa, one can view it as prophecy. In the penal colony on a tropical island, an explorer is being shown by an officer the apparatus used for executing criminals. It is a fiendish machine consisting of a bed on which the condemned man is placed naked and strapped down, while an ingenious contrivance of needles above him writes the sentence upon his body. The procedure is geared to a slow pace so that death comes only after twelve hours of torture:

". . . So that the actual progress of the sentence can be watched, the Harrow is made of glass. Getting the

[6] *PS*, p. 82.

K C

needles fixed in the glass was a technical problem, but after many experiments we overcame the difficulty. No trouble was too great for us to take, you see. And now anyone can look through the glass and watch the inscription taking form on the body. . . ."[7]

There is even a water spray to wash away the blood and keep the inscription clear.

The machine had been invented by a former Commandant of the colony, now dead. The new Commandant disapproves of the machine whose only supporter is the officer who describes it so lovingly to the explorer. When the explorer expresses his horror and condemnation of the contrivance, the officer releases the prisoner whose execution was about to take place, and ecstatically places himself on the machine. "Be just" is the inscription that pierces him.

This allegory bears certain similarities to *The Judgment*. The machine itself is as infallible as the father was in the earlier story. But in addition to the two opposing attitudes, father and son in *The Judgment*, old harsh régime and new humane one in *In the Penal Settlement*, we now have an impartial observer as well, in the figure of the explorer. Yet even he, in the end, does not question the Kafka axiom that guilt is unquestionable. The prisoner condemned to die in the machine never actually knows the verdict. He realises the sentence completely only when it is etched upon his body by the needles. This we are told in obscene detail:

". . . The first six hours the condemned man stays alive almost as before, he suffers only pain. After two hours the felt gag is taken away, for he has no longer strength to scream. Here, into this electrically heated basin at the head of the Bed, some warm rice-pap is poured, from which the man, if he feels like it, can take as much as his tongue can lap. Not one of them ever

[7] *PS*, p. 194.

misses the chance. I can remember none, and my experience is extensive. Only about the sixth hour does the man lose all desire to eat. I usually kneel down here at that moment and observe the phenomenon. The man rarely swallows his last mouthful, he only rolls it round his mouth and spits it out into the grave. I have to duck just then or he would spit it in my face. But how quiet he grows at just about the sixth hour! Enlightenment comes to the most dull-witted. It begins around the eyes. From there it radiates. A moment that might tempt one to get under the Harrow with him. Nothing more happens after that, the man only begins to understand the inscription, he purses his mouth as if he were listening. You have seen how difficult it is to decipher the script with one's eyes; but our man deciphers it with his wounds. To be sure, that is a hard task; he needs six hours to accomplish it. By that time the Harrow has pierced him quite through and casts him into the grave, where he pitches down upon the blood and water and the cotton-wool. Then the judgment has been fulfilled, and we, the soldier and I, bury him."[8]

It would be pointless for the prisoner to be allowed to defend himself at his trial, since he would only lie. He is guilty. Mankind is guilty, so Christian doctrine asserts. And indeed it is as a series of Christian symbols that the disgusting machine can be most suitably viewed. The whole business of execution parallels life governed by Christianity. The inventor of the machine, the old Commandant, is probably God. Although he is dead, there are rumours in the colony that he will come again.

The absolute disgust with life which gives *In the Penal Settlement* its predominant odour increasingly pervades Kafka's later stories and fables, though not always in as direct and potent a form. The collection entitled *A Country Doctor* consists of fourteen short stories which Kafka collected and published in 1919 with a dedication to his father. Each of these brief pieces has its own fascination, and in them Kafka's artistry can be clearly perceived and appreciated. The stories are of various kinds, though the majority are written in the form of first-person narrative. Sometimes they are no more than two or three hundred words, as is the first piece, "The New Advocate." The story which gives the collection its title is a more complex affair. The country doctor who narrates the tale is called out to a patient during a blizzard. His horse had died, so he uses two horses which have mysteriously appeared with an unknown groom. He reaches his patient, a young man who whispers "Doctor, let me die,"[9] and who is found to be suffering from an incurable wound. The young man's family, obeying some old superstitious rite, strip the doctor of his clothes and place him in bed with the youth, hoping thus to effect a cure. The doctor talks to the patient, then flees. The wound may be despair, the doctor's nakedness his spiritual condition. He is powerless to help the youth, and the quasi-erotic comfort suggested by the curious undressing motif is the only relief he can offer.

This strange tale is written in Kafka's most careful and balanced prose, as is the following piece, "Up in the Gallery" which, though no more than a couple of paragraphs long, has an architectural structure which is rich and complex in the interrelation of its parts. In "An Old Manuscript," one of Kafka's obsessive subjects reappears: the necessary ubiquitousness of evil. Evil, this time, is personified by a horde of nomads who quietly infiltrate into a town one night and are not to be got rid of. "Before the Law" adumbrates the theme of *The Castle*, and actually appears again in *The Trial*, and "Jackals and Arabs," one of the most complex and extraordinary tales

[9] *PS*, p. 134.

in the collection, is a bitter essay on the paradoxical nature of the human condition.

"A Visit to a Mine" shares with the other stories an almost cinematic realism in the telling and an opaque, dream-like quality in what is being told. Plato's image of the cave throws no more light on our fears and our possibilities than this. There are only two sentences in "The Next Village," but they are so pregnant not with meaning but with the possibility of development and exegesis that their impact is that of a long and solid dissertation.

"A Message from the Emperor" (which is also to be found embedded in *The Great Wall of China*) is the quietly desperate cry of an agnostic yearning for a faith his reason will not allow him to accept. It is hardly more than a page long, yet the chilling wind of despair whistles through it more surely than through the various meretricious novellas it has inspired over the years. That spiritual emptiness which a decade or two later was to become the fashionable stock-in-trade of the "serious" Catholic novelist was to Kafka a dread reality.

One of the most curious fragments in *A Country Doctor* is "Troubles of a Householder" which, perhaps more determinedly than any other short piece by Kafka, foreshadows the absurdist theatre of Ionesco and, more particularly, Pinter. The householder has really only one trouble: a ridiculous, unwanted guest in his house. Not even a guest, since there exists great doubt as to whether he or it is alive. Though it does move.

At first glance it looks like a flat star-shaped spool for thread, and indeed it does seem to have thread wound upon it; to be sure, only old, broken-off bits of thread are eligible, not merely knotted but tangled together, of the most varied sorts and colours. But it is not only a spool, for a small wooden cross-bar sticks out of the middle of the star, and another small rod is joined to that at a right angle. By means of this latter rod on one side and one of the points of the star on the other, the whole thing can stand upright as if on two legs.[10]

When asked its name, it replies "Odradek." The householder muses on whether this word is of Slavonic or German origin. (He does not realise, apparently, that in Czech the word means something like "outside the law.") Odradek is purposeless, senseless. He does no harm, he causes no great inconvenience, "but," says the householder, "the idea that he is likely to survive me I find almost painful."[11]

In considering Odradek's meaningless existence, the householder is facing the senselessness of his own life. Odradek serves no purpose but his own inscrutable one. Perhaps man's predicament is similar. Perhaps he, too, is a law unto himself, devoid of objective meaning. "One is tempted to believe that the creature once had some sort of intelligible shape and is now only a broken-down remnant."[12] Tempted indeed, for if one once had meaning, purpose, innocence, then perhaps one day one might regain these qualities. The superstitious doctrine of original sin both torments and soothes the householder, but reason forces him to admit that there is no sign of Odradek's once having served any purpose, no evidence to support even so bleak a reassurance as this.

"Eleven Sons" begins with the sentence "I have eleven sons." The next eleven paragraphs describe each of them in turn. The final sentence is "These are my eleven sons." The sons, however, are clearly aspects of the writer's own personality, or indications of directions in which his personality might develop. It is not without interest, though it lacks the irony and complexity of thought of many of its companion pieces. These are qualities displayed with abundant virtuosity in the

[10] *PS*, pp. 156-7.   [11] *PS*, p. 158.   [12] *PS*, p. 157.

following story, "A Brother's Murder," which lends itself to so wide a variety of interpretations that it is almost more meaningful to consider it as a beautiful piece of pure music, unable, by its very nature, to refer to anything outside itself. The subject-matter of this extraordinary prose poem is, so to speak, irrelevant. Something of the same feeling could have been achieved had Schmar, the murderer, committed instead some act other than that of fratricide. The moonlit detail of the observation, the creative joy that wells up in the telling of the tale, the dionysiac ecstasy of the *acte gratuite*, the unnervingly brilliant arrangement of the narrative, all these qualities clamour together to partially obscure the deeper significance and resonance of Schmar's involuntary gesture. This is the nearest Kafka will approach to the light-hearted *Credo* of a Mozart Mass. It is belief seen through a window whose glass may or may not distort.

Schmar's sudden movement towards self-fulfilment is, as such, a failure. In "A Dream," it is the consciousness of this failure that lures Schmar, or Josef K. as he has now become, literally into his grave. This simple, chilling death-wish dream is a clear and unsentimental expression of K.'s quiet self-pity. In his dream he finds himself in a cemetery, on his knees before a freshly-dug grave. An artist arrives to carve an inscription on the blank tombstone. As he sees his own name scrawled on the stone, K. sinks peacefully into the earth.

Fulfilment is impossible, failure is too easy. There remain adaptation, compromise, conformity; and it is with a savageness tempered by irony that Kafka gives us a classical account of these ploys of the ordinary man, in "A Report to an Academy." "Honoured members of the Academy," it begins, "You have done me the honour of inviting me to give your Academy an account of the life I formerly led as an ape."[13] The bitter comedy of this report by the ape who has managed to escape confine-

[13] *PS*, p. 169.

ment in a cage by apeing at first the mannerisms and finally the desires of mankind, is more explicit and closer to the surface than is usually the case with Kafka. "With an effort which up till now has never been repeated," reports the ex-ape, "I managed to reach the cultural level of an average European. In itself that might be nothing to speak of, but it is something in so far as it has helped me out of my cage and opened a special way out for me, the way of humanity."[14] We achieve success in life (and the limited success of getting out of the cage is all we can really hope for) by imitating those who would keep us caged. We may occasionally feel the breeze at our heels, or be unable to look one of our as yet only half-trained fellow-creatures in the eye, but it is nevertheless the only convenient and comfortable way to exist. Of course, if convenience and comfort are not the most important things in the world to us, then we are already equipped to find another way out of the cage. But it is not, implies Kafka, the majority way.

The Country Doctor, then, contains riches out of all proportion to its brevity. Amongst the remainder of Kafka's shorter fiction, there are a few other unfinished pieces, some quite long, others mere fragments, that require to be considered. "Blumenfield, an Elderly Bachelor," for instance, which could almost be some anti-Kafkaite satirist's comment on *The Trial*. The punctilious, orderly clerk Blumenfield is plagued by two balls which bounce up and down behind him and cannot be got rid of. One's first ribald comment might well be that they represent sex rearing its ugly heads. But it does not matter what particular aspects of the instinctual or the unconscious the balls represent. That they are messengers from a distant, repressed world is obvious; that they are not extraneous terrors but legitimate aspects of a personality longing for integration is cunningly and wittily conveyed by Kafka.

[14] *PS*, p. 180.

Only a fragment remains of *The Great Wall of China*. Brod suggests that Kafka completed the work but destroyed the final version. The portion that exists employs easily deciphered symbolism in considering the problems of perfection and human society. Several other fragmentary episodes written during 1918-19 may well have been intended as sections of *The Great Wall of China*. In some cases one can deduce quite easily that such is the case. "The Conscription of Troops," for instance, though probably written later, is a description of a curious Chinese custom whose meaning is not easy to fathom. Nor does the story yield itself immediately to interpretation. Its theme is fulfilment of identity and of purpose. When a woman hears that there is to be a conscription of troops, it is the custom for her to travel to the house where the conscription is to take place. At first she is received ceremoniously, but when the officer who is conscripting the troops arrives, she is forced to flee in shame.

"The Refusal" was probably also a part of *The Great Wall of China*. Certainly it inhabits the same emotional world as "The Conscription of Troops," though there is no indication that the town "far from the frontier" where the events take place is Chinese. Indeed it is more likely that the townspeople, who regularly approach the highest local official with a request which is as regularly refused, are in fact a Jewish tribe. The prayers of Israel for deliverance from exile were not heard by Jehovah.

Of more abiding interest are the stories collected in 1924 under the title *A Hunger Artist*. These stories, written near the end of Kafka's life, are still as ironic in tone as most of the earlier ones, but they differ in being lighter in some way, in being in some curious manner life-enhancing. The point must not be too heavily stressed, for there is nothing of facile optimism in these strange tales. What there is is a perceptible though slight change of viewpoint, almost a prophetic serenity.

The first of these four stories, "First Sorrow," tells of a trapeze artist who spends almost his entire life high up on his trapeze. Even when the other acts are performing on the stage, he continues to sit up there awaiting his turn. The inevitable journeys from town to town were managed by the fastest of cars so that he could get aloft again as soon as possible. He becomes dissatisfied with his one bar, and asks his manager to install another. This absurd, life-denying concentration in perfecting his craft has its parallel in Kafka's intense preoccupation with the problem of being a writer. As the trapeze artist's manager feared when acceding to the request for another bar:

> Once such ideas began to torment him, would they ever quite leave him alone? Would they not rather increase in urgency? Would they not threaten his very existence? And indeed the manager believed he could see, during the apparently peaceful sleep which had succeeded the fit of tears, the first furrows of care engraving themselves upon the trapeze artist's smooth, child-like forehead.[15]

In "A Little Woman" the narrator reflects on his next-door neighbour, a slim, tightly-laced little woman, who cannot stand him and who is continually in a state of hysteria about him. His apparently calm and urbane acceptance of her non-acceptance of him, despite the fact that he admits to having become somewhat uneasy about it over the past ten years, reveals a state of equilibrium unusual for Kafka's "I" figures.

But the finest of these stories is undoubtedly the one which gives its name to the collection. The hunger artist himself, renowned for his forty-day fasts in a circus cage, is no artist at all. His dying confession is that he fasted only because he could never find food that he liked. "If I had found any, believe me, I should have made no bones about it and stuffed myself like you or anyone else."[16] He

[15] *PS*, p. 228.   [16] *PS*, p. 249.

would have died, true to himself, several years earlier had not his impresario forced him to eat between engagements. It is only when his act falls from favour, and he has to function without an impresario, that he is able to achieve the complete self-fulfilment which, for him, means death. It is, Kafka seems to say, the built-in impresario in each of us which keeps us alive and bitterly fraudulent. But the fraud we practise, or more properly speaking the fraud practised by the tragic artist, is of a different nature to the fraud that the artist's public suspects is being practised upon them. The tragic artist whose masterpiece is greeted with the unfeeling Philistine cry "Things aren't really as bad as all that," has no defence, can call no witnesses. He himself knows both that things aren't that bad and that they are much, much worse. The real problem can never be shared: to each his own. But whether one starves because one wills one's death, or because one cannot find food that one can endure, whatever the exact nature of one's secret, one will carry it, misunderstood, to one's grave. Of such is the kingdom of man.

The last story is "Josephine the Singer, or the Mouse-Folk." Josephine is the only singer in the nation of mice. She likes to sing at times of national emergency. Kafka's mice-folk, surely, are the Jewish race, while Josephine herself is prophecy, theology, or perhaps a personification of the people's faith in God.

But from that point it is a long, long way to Josephine's claim that she gives us new strength and so on and so forth. For ordinary people, at least, not for her train of flatterers. "What other explanation could there be?"—they say with quite shameless sauciness—"How else could you explain the great audiences, especially when danger is most imminent, which have even often enough hindered proper precautions being taken in time to avert danger." Now, this last statement is unfortunately true, but can hardly be counted as one of Josephine's titles to fame, especially considering that when such large gatherings have been unexpectedly flushed by the enemy and many of our people left lying for dead, Josephine, who was responsible for it all, and, indeed, perhaps attracted the enemy by her piping, has always occupied the safest place and was always the first to whisk away quietly and speedily under cover of her escort.[17]

So it is certain that Josephine's career has passed its zenith. The thought gives rise to no sadness in this delightful yet moving parable.

Problems of the same kind are at the core of "The Giant Mole," the story of an old village schoolmaster's discovery of a huge mole and his absurd hopes of the fame that will accrue to him because of it. The narrator is a businessman who, not in the least intrigued by the mole, busies himself in the matter out of sympathy for the schoolmaster, and writes a pamphlet in a futile attempt to rouse an apathetic public to some degree of interest in the discovery. Whether one sees the giant mole as religious belief, or liberal opinion or any more particular cause is of no great importance. The finally pointless relationship of the committed person, the schoolmaster, and the well-meaning, free-thinking observer, the businessman, is examined with a lively humour. Fanaticism and intelligent interest, suspicious of each other, are both defeated by indifference.

One of the most curiously beautiful of Kafka's final stories is "Investigations of a Dog." It may, in fact, have been the very last story he wrote. In it, one meets again the principal themes that obsessed Kafka all his life: the uncertainty of existence, the necessity of the continual search for truth and the knowledge that such a search is fruitless, the idea of redemption, the validity of mystical

[17] *PS*, p. 264.

experience. The pity and irony implied by the brilliant stroke of making the investigator a dog, and thus limited by his dogginess are never overstressed, or indeed stressed at all. The aesthetic fact is enough. When the dog, forlorn and starving, is at the point of death, he encounters a beautiful hunting dog who refuses to let him lie in the forest, and then appears to be preparing to sing:

> "You're going to sing," I said. "Yes," he replied gravely, "I'm going to sing soon, but not yet." "You're beginning already," I said. "No," he said, "not yet. But be prepared." "I can hear it already, though you deny it," I said, trembling. He was silent, and then I thought I saw something such as no dog before me had ever seen, at least there is no slightest hint of it in our tradition, and I hastily bowed my head in infinite fear and shame in the pool of blood lying before me. I thought I saw that the hound was already singing without knowing it nay, more, that the melody, separated from him, was floating on the air in accordance with its own laws, and, as though he had no part in it, was moving towards me, towards me alone.[18]

This strange experience, an intimation of immortality or of the life of the spirit, was perhaps real, perhaps an illusion. Or a delirium induced by the investigator's weakened condition. His physical recovery was rapid, but a part of his spirit that was touched by the experience bore the marks forever. The dog, or Kafka, or the individual seeking to understand his predicament, will never understand it other than momentarily. The moment of perception is, after all, a moment. Otherwise, life would be even less bearable.

In an editorial comment on "The Burrow," a story Kafka wrote in the last year of his life, Max Brod writes:

[18] *DS*, p. 286.

. . . the reader should pay attention to the important passage where the author, usually so careful to avoid any abstract statement, lifts the veil a little and hints that "The Burrow" means more to him than mere security: it means a home and a life founded on honest work—in short, the very things for which the surveyor K. in *The Castle* searched in vain.[19]

This apparently innocuous remark is indicative of Brod's general attitude to Kafka and of the often solicitous nature of his interpretation of the author. But, however sentimentally reassuring it might be to think of Kafka snug in his little Berlin burrow with Dora, "The Burrow" is, alas, saying something quite different. Kafka was sentimental neither about others nor about himself. "The Burrow" is a work of bitterness, despair, self-condemnation, pessimism and fear. As published, it is incomplete. The complete version ended with the collapse of the burrow and the defeat of its occupant by an enemy. The enemy, as we know now and no doubt Kafka knew at the time, is death. This richly symbolic story tells us many things, but is is, after all, a work of art and not an *apologia pro sua vita*. We can deduce much from it, but what we can deduce is nothing like the accept-ance, reconciliation and final calm that Brod would appear to insist upon. The nervous, frightened, lonely animal in its cunningly constructed burrow can hear the enemy outside. His defences are futile and he awaits the inevitable. His security, achieved at great cost, is nothing. The rational, constructed world is at the mercy of dark, irrational forces. The rational is temporal, the irrational is eternal. This dark, pessimistic, almost tragic picture of the human predicament leaves one with a feeling not of sentimental warmth but of gloomy help-lessness.

Kafka's monumental despair is most moving when it

19 *DS*, p. 342.

is given a series of objective correlatives. To read some of the more intensely self-absorbed entries in the diaries and notebooks, such as "8th. December. Bed, constipation, pain in back, irritable evening, cat in the room, dissension"[20] nowadays is to invite mirth. There are borderline cases, of course, entries which were later to be expanded and metamorphosed into works of art. Some of them are invented, imagined, some of them may be dreams. Kafka's inner dream-life was an immensely fruitful one, and he drew on it shrewdly. He was also aware, as Goethe was, that true wisdom consists in knowing that "against the superiority of others there exists no weapon or remedy save that of love." The brief jottings in the Notebooks are often born of love for himself. From them, he constructed works of art and of love for others: the stories and, above all else, the three novels *America*, *The Trial* and *The Castle*.

[20] *WP*, p. 88.

CHAPTER IV

AMERICA

While he was writing "The Stoker," the first chapter of *America*, Kafka made this entry in his diary:

> Dickens' *Copperfield*. "The Stoker" a sheer imitation of Dickens, the projected novel even more so. The story of the trunk, the boy who delights and charms everyone, the menial labour, his sweetheart in the country house, the dirty houses et al., but above all the method. It was my intention, as I now see, to write a Dickens novel, but enhanced by the sharper lights I have taken from the times and the duller ones I should have got from myself. Dickens' opulence and great, careless prodigality, but in consequence passages of awful insipidity, in which he wearily works over effects he has already achieved. Gives one a barbaric impression because the whole does not make sense, a barbarism that I, it is true, thanks to my weakness and wiser for my epigonism, have been able to avoid. There is a heartlessness behind his sentimentally over-flowing style. These rude characterisations which are artificially stamped on everyone and without which Dickens would not be able to get on with his story even for a moment.[1]

We can get from this some idea of what Kafka *thought* he was doing in *America*. A surface realism, or the deceptive appearance of realism in the novel, certainly owes a debt to Dickens, and also creates a gulf in style between *America* and the two other novels. But as one studies

[1] *DFK*, Vol. 2, pp. 188-9.

America one soon comes to see not only that Kafka's methods are widely dissimilar from Dickens', but that his real intent lies in a different direction from that of the English novelist.

The Castle and *The Trial* are set in a strange country of the soul, which may occasionally resemble the Bohemia of the Austro-Hungarian Empire, but which more often corresponds to the dark townscapes of Kafka's dreams. *America*, on the other hand, is set in the United States of America. Or rather in Kafka's conception of that country which he never visited. It is, of course, an imaginary America, as any other novelist's is. It is also the imagined America of a central European and, as such, has strong affinities with Brecht's Mahagonny. At night, it is the Moon of Alabama that gleams over Kafka's scene. Even so, something of the quality of Kafka's crumbling Austro-Hungarian world has found its way into this curious land, particularly in the characters by whom it is peopled.

The picaresque construction of *America* makes it easier to read than the other, more densely complex novels. The hero of *America*, Karl Rossmann, is a sixteen-year-old, whereas the K.s of the other novels are over thirty. They are more complicated creatures than the young Karl.

In *America*, Karl's attempts to find a working relationship between innocence and freedom are described with a relative lightness and objectivity. As Kafka informs us in his opening sentence, Karl Rossmann has been "packed off to America by his parents because a servant girl had seduced him and got herself with child by him."[2] In the first chapter, called "The Stoker," Karl's ship arrives in New York harbour as a sudden burst of sunshine illuminates the Statue of Liberty. He is about to leave the ship when he realises he has forgotten his umbrella. Leaving his trunk with a casual acquaintance he makes his way down into the bowels of the ship, opens

[2] *A*, p. 13.

the wrong door and so meets a stoker. He becomes obsessed with this man's various grievances, and goes with him to the Captain to help him to enforce his rights. The justice meted out in the Captain's room, however, is of the most technical kind. Human considerations are unknown. Everything else is subjugated to organisation. Discipline is, in fact, more relevant to the situation than justice. Karl has been of no real help to the stoker, and when he finally leaves the ship with his uncle, the Senator, "it was now as if there were really no stoker at all."[3]

The fact that the construction of *America* is so much looser in both form and texture than either *The Castle* or *The Trial* has led some commentators to the view that it is an altogether lighter work than the other two novels. Even its co-translator, Edwin Muir, in his Introduction to the English edition, writes: "*America* is one of the happiest of Kafka's stories. In his other two long stories the fantasy is never far from nightmare; but here, except in the description of the country house and of Delamarche's quarters with Brunelda, it is pure enjoyment, free improvisation without any or without much serious afterthought."[4]

It is foolhardy to assume that anything by Kafka is meant to have no significance, and surely even a casual reading of *America* convinces one that here Kafka was making a quite deliberate attempt to create a character experiencing and grappling with a strange world. It is a more externalised world than that of *The Trial* or *The Castle*, or rather it necessarily seems so to its extremely youthful protagonist. But although, because of this, *America* may appear to lack the ambiguity of those other works, it is nevertheless concerned with the same themes, and concerned with them just as seriously as are the more obviously obsessive novels.

The second of the eight almost self-contained chapters

[3] *A*, p. 48.   [4] *A*, pp. 7-8.

concentrates on Uncle Jacob who had emigrated to America more than thirty years earlier and was now an immensely successful business man. He is equally concerned with being an American and with making a good American of his nephew. He gives Karl a room on the sixth floor of his house which is also his place of business. The narrow balcony of Karl's room looks down into a busy New York Street, and Uncle Jacob warns him not to be beguiled by it. He himself had known newcomers, for example, who, instead of following wise precepts, had stood all day on their balconies gaping down at the street like lost sheep! This was no way to behave in the land of opportunity.

Karl is set to learning English very quickly, and made to have riding-lessons so early every morning that he has to get up at half-past four. When Mr Pollunder, a banker and business acquaintance of Uncle Jacob's, invites Karl to his country house, Karl's uncle reacts in a curious mixture of formality, reluctance and impatience. His own life is empty, determined, business-like and, he would say, practical. For Karl to be successful in his eyes, he must come to adopt Uncle Jacob's attitudes, and become the same kind of monster. But monsters are a threat to one another, so there are moments when Uncle Jacob harks back to a time of pre-business kindness; when he, grudgingly, allows Karl to play the piano, asking if he would perhaps not like to learn the violin or the horn as well. Possibly this methodical business-man uncle could have become Karl's saviour, severe, just and decisive. As it is, his role in shaping Karl's character appears somewhat ambiguous. Uncle Jacob strives towards an ideal, while Karl's behaviour is always related to the real world. There are ethical systems by which the uncle's way of life would be judged good, and Karl's evil. And *vice versa*. Kafka deliberately gnaws away at the hopelessness of attaining any real insight, any knowledge of the one inner truth.

The third chapter takes place in Mr Pollunder's country house outside New York, where Karl spends a very peculiar evening. On arriving, he meets Pollunder's daughter Clara, and is disturbed to find that another business friend of his uncle's, Mr Green, has unexpectedly turned up. After an uneasy dinner, Karl is taken upstairs by Clara who becomes increasingly irritable until she eventually fights Karl, and beats him. After various adventures, Karl not surprisingly decides to leave, but is prevented from doing so by Green who says he has some important news for Karl at midnight. This turns out to be a letter from his uncle, addressed "To Karl Ross-mann, to be delivered personally at midnight, wherever he may be found." Because Karl chose to spend the night at Pollunder's house, his uncle will have nothing further to do with him:

> . . . I must, after the incident of today, expressly send you away from me, and I urgently beg you neither to visit me in person, nor to try to get in touch with me by either writing or through intermediaries. Against my wishes you decided this evening to leave me; stick, then, to that decision all your life. Only then will it be a manly decision.[5]

Uncle Jacob had, in fact, given a reluctant kind of permission for the visit, though he made his disapproval clear. Pollunder's charm and kindness had won Karl over, and made his uncle's disapproval temporarily appear harmless. To Uncle Jacob, nevertheless, this was no ordinary social visit; and indeed Karl's evening at Pollunder's house was quite an extraordinary one. The house itself was odd: an old-fashioned building, only parts of which were habitable. Pollunder himself is pleasant, easy-going, a superficial character unlikely to explore his own darker side, and content to live with the furnished, conscious top layer of his mind. To

[5] *A*, p. 103.

Pollunder his house is not unusual, nor can anything out of the ordinary happen in it. Karl's experience of it is on an altogether deeper level of awareness.

It appears that the house really belongs to the rich young Mack, Karl's riding instructor, who is now revealed to be Clara's fiancé. Mack is an uncomplicated, sunny character to whom the world is a busy and happy place. He has neither cares nor suspicions: he is devoted to happiness. He provides a more positive, and wounding, contrast to Karl than Mr Pollunder does. When Karl plays the piano for Clara, he feels strange aspirations and longings within him and then is overcome with a sense of his own inadequacy. Mack, hearing him play, senses nothing of this. He notices a few mistakes, but nevertheless is greatly pleased by the performance. His greatest capacity is for enjoyment.

Various forces combine to complete the separation of Karl from his uncle. Pollunder dissuades him from taking the night train back. Green actually tricks him into staying till midnight so that delivery of the uncle's letter will be more easily and conveniently accomplished. Karl's disobedience to his uncle could have been forgiven. If he and his uncle had been the only persons involved, perhaps it would have been. But the senseless interference of the intermediary Green gives the act an importance and a consequence both of which were unforeseen. Karl is now expelled from his uncle's stern but benevolent protection, and thrust out into the world. Green presents him with a third-class ticket to San Francisco, adding: "In Frisco you can tackle anything you like; just begin at the bottom and trying gradually to work your way up."[6]

Karl detects no malice in these words, and surely there is none. Green's function is to hinder, perhaps to destroy, almost inadvertently, through his own shortcomings rather than by any active malevolence. He represents

[6] *A*, pp. 104-5.

that senseless, coincidental aspect of existence which can so vitally yet capriciously affect even the most perfectly planned endeavours. Karl is now completely on his own, and responsible only to himself. He selects a direction by chance, and sets out on his way.

The fourth chapter, "The Road to Rameses," begins with Karl's arrival at a lorry-driver's roadside inn. It is not yet dawn, and when he asks for the cheapest bed to be had he is shown by an old hag into a room with two beds on which two young men are sleeping, fully dressed. Karl falls asleep in a chair, and in the morning meets the two vagrants, an Irishman called Robinson, and a Frenchman, Delamarche. They claim to be mechanics who had lost their jobs in New York and were travelling to the small town of Butterford where it was rumoured that work was to be had. They offer to take Karl with them, and he is gullible enough to agree. They are hustled out of the room by the old woman and, after a foul breakfast consisting solely of a can of coffee which they are obliged to pass from mouth to mouth, they take to the road.

A truck passes slowly, with a sign on it: "Dock labourers wanted by the Jacob Despatch Agency." This is Karl's uncle's firm. But Robinson and Delamarche are, of course, really looking for anything but work. They scornfully refuse the invitation to work for Uncle Jacob, saying that his organisation is notorious throughout the United States. Walking on, they reach a hill from which they look back on New York and its harbour. Karl has a momentary urge to return there, but is persuaded to go on to Butterford or even, if no work is to be had there, to California to look for gold. Such an idea is typical of the way the two shiftless characters plan, or rather fail to plan, their actions. They want simply to exist, without effort and without work. If they are criminal, it is only because they are sometimes forced to be, by immediate hunger. They are not thieves, they are not vicious, but they are selfish, lazy and irresponsible because their view of the world is childish and superficial. Somewhere within themselves, they are possessed of the unconscious knowledge that this is so, and it is this that motivates their dazed and inarticulate contempt for the precision and order represented by Uncle Jacob and his firm, which they can dimly perceive constitutes a threat to their own sub-idyllic existence.

They stop for lunch, and Karl has to pay for their meal. In the evening they rest by the wayside, and Karl is sent to a nearby hotel to bring food back to them. While he is away, the two men break open the box he has left behind. He returns to find the box open and a photograph of his parents missing. Distressed at losing the photograph, he offers the men the contents of the box for it, but they claim not to have seen it. For them, such an object as a photograph is so unimportant, so insignificant that they probably have not noticed it.

The relationship between Karl and the two tramps is so incompatible and so fruitless that it begins rapidly to disintegrate. While Karl had been waiting at the hotel bar for food, he had met an elderly woman who was clearly a member of the staff. In fact, she is the Manager-ess. It was she who took him to the kitchen and gave him the bacon, bread and beer that he had been told to obtain. She invites Karl, and the companions he has mentioned, to stay overnight in the hotel, but Karl is by now ashamed of the other two and refuses. Nevertheless, the incident of the photograph makes Karl determined to part company with Robinson and Delamarche, and when the Manageress sends a waiter across from the hotel to invite them again to stay, Karl accepts the invitation and leaves his two companions.

In Chapter four, "The Hotel Occidental," we find that Karl and the Manageress are fellow-countrymen. She comes from Vienna, and had once worked at a hotel in Prague. On the strength of this, she offers Karl a

job as lift-boy, pointing out to him that he will undoubtedly be able to work his way up. Karl has no
scruples about accepting so menial a post. After all, he
is in a new country where his European education is
virtually meaningless. Besides, "Karl had always admired
lift-boys; he thought them very ornamental."[7] This is
the first overt suggestion in the novel that Karl has the
slightest homosexual inclination: it is a suggestion that is
to grow stronger until Karl's sexual attitudes are finally,
if by no means unequivocally, resolved at the end of the
book. But once the thought has been placed in the
reader's mind, he is inclined to ponder on the real
meaning of Karl's earlier relationships. The remark
about the lift-boys is in one sense misleading. It suggests
a masculine attraction for the pretty and the ornamental. But if Karl is to any degree homosexually inclined, he is passively and masochistically so, and his
interest is in older, stronger men than himself. Father-
figures, in fact. And as soon as one begins to view him in
this light, Karl takes on unexpected similarities to the
young Kafka of the "Letter to his Father." It is possible
to consider *America* in its entirety as the account of a
struggle to escape from the father-figure and, by extension, of Karl's struggles to free himself from his homosexual masochistic leanings and to achieve a more
accepted and therefore acceptable heterosexual way of
life. Karl's first American encounter, one remembers,
was with the ship's stoker. "The stoker seems to have
bewitched you,"[8] his uncle had said. "Seduced" might
have been a more appropriate word. After all, when
Karl had knocked on his door "by mistake," the stoker
had almost immediately dragged him into his cabin, and
a moment later was inviting him to lie down in his bunk.

Karl's relationship with Uncle Jacob has been merely
a more sophisticated enacting of his attitude to the stoker.
The stoker was physically a huge man, we are told.

[7] *A*, p. 143.   [8] *A*, p. 45.

Uncle Jacob is big in importance, in wealth. Almost all
the other men, including the rich young Mack and the
two vagrants, exist in a curiously ambivalent relationship
to Karl, whose lack of sexual balance may well relate to
Kafka's own efforts at this time of his life (*c.* 1912) to
find some form of emotional equilibrium. True, Karl had
been sent to America as the result of a liaison of some
kind with a servant, but she had been older than he,
had obviously been the active partner, and was bearing
a child which she was probably only trying to pass off
as his.

Karl's new friend the Manageress takes him to an
attic room which is part of her own suite. Her secretary,
a European girl called Therese who sleeps in an adjoining
room, comes in later and talks to Karl. Next day he is
pitched into the world of the lift-boys. He moves into
their dormitory.

As a quiet place to sleep in, the dormitory certainly
left much to be desired. For each boy had his own time-
table for eating, sleeping, recreation and incidental
services during his free twelve hours; so that the place
was always in a turmoil. Some would be lying asleep
with blankets pulled over their ears to deaden noises,
and if one of them were roused he would yell with such
fury about the din made by the rest that all the other
sleepers, no matter how soundly they slept, were bound
to waken up. Almost every boy had a pipe, which was
indulged in as a sort of luxury, and Karl got himself
one too and soon acquired a taste for it. Now smoking
was of course forbidden on duty, and the consequence
was that in the dormitory everyone smoked if he was not
actually asleep. As a result, each bed stood in its own
smoke cloud and the whole room was enveloped in a
general haze.[9]

The chaos of the lift-boys' dormitory is at any rate

[9] *A*, p. 157.

reality of a kind, whereas the hotel's façade of life is emptily formal, meaninglessly semi-polite, and takes no account of the disorder beneath the surface. It is not surprising that, through this disorder, Karl should be led back into contact with the near-tramps Robinson and Delamarche. The handsomest of the lift-boys, an American youth named Rennell (of whom it was rumoured "that a fashionable lady who had been staying in the hotel for some time had kissed him, to say the least of it, in the lift"[10]) tells Karl that a man called Delamarche had stopped him one day outside the hotel and questioned him about Karl. And, in the following chapter, "The Case of Robinson," Robinson suddenly turns up while Karl is on duty at his lift.

Although Delamarche has been mentioned by the handsome lift-boy (and there is a faint suggestion that the boy Rennell has perhaps been spending his nights with Delamarche: he was "no longer to be seen in the dormitory. No other boy had so completely deserted the community of the lift-boys. . . . All this flashed through Karl's mind, together with reflections on Delamarche",)[11] it is Robinson alone who has come to entice Karl away from the hotel. He is badly but quite expensively dressed, and is out to make an impression:

"Wouldn't you like to come and see us, Rossmann. We're living in great style now," said Robinson, leering seductively at Karl.

"Does the invitation come from you or from Delamarche?" asked Karl.

"From me and Delamarche. Both of us together," said Robinson.[12]

He is drunk, and within a few moments is being heartily sick in the stair-well. Feeling sorry for him, Karl takes him up to the dormitory, where

[10] *A*, p. 168.   [11] *A*, pp. 168-9.   [12] *A*, p. 172.

the majority lay on their backs staring at the roof, while here and there a boy, clothed or unclothed as he chanced to be, sprang out of bed to see how things were going at the other end of the room. So Karl managed to guide Robinson who had now become somewhat used to walking, as far as Rennell's bed without rousing much attention, for the bed was quite near the door and luckily unoccupied; in his own bed, as he could see from the distance, a strange boy whom he did not know was quietly sleeping.[13]

Why does Karl put Robinson in Rennell's bed? Robinson has a few moments earlier told him that Rennell is with Delamarche and that it was really both of them who had sent him to see Karl. The confused sexual overtones multiply.

It is discovered that Karl has been absent from his lift and that he has brought a drunken man into the dormitory. The Head Waiter and the Head Porter hold a summary court of inquiry and, despite the Manageress's admittedly somewhat half-hearted defence of him, Karl is dismissed. The justice meted out to him is as much a travesty as that suffered by the stoker in the very first chapter. European concern for truth is irrelevant: in America the machine is master, and throws out what it cannot absorb smoothly. As long as discipline is systematic, it has no need to be just. For "America" read "the surface life."

Is Karl offering Robinson to Rennell as a vicarious substitute for himself? Or is he subconsciously attempting to implicate Rennell and discredit him? What, for that matter, is the significance of the unknown boy sleeping in Karl's bed? He can surely be nothing other than an incarnation, an externalisation of Karl's own repressed desires. Here, it seems, Kafka has lost control and is distributing bodies in beds with careless abandon.

[13] *A*, p. 177.

America constantly veers between realism and fantasy. At this point we are indulging in fantasy. Now realism temporarily takes over.

Out in the street, Karl finds the recuperating Robinson awaiting him. With the help of a couple of lift-boys, he manages to get Robinson into a taxi and they go off to Robinson and Delamarche's suburban apartment. Here Karl makes the acquaintance of Brunelda. But before considering what in the English Definitive Edition are the last two chapters of *America*, we ought at this point to give some thought to just how closely the published work fairly represents Kafka's intentions. Brod, in a Postscript to the work, after describing it as "more optimistic and lighter in mood than any of [Kafka's] other writings,"[14] asserts that the author suddenly stopped work on the novel before he had completed it, but that the incomplete chapter called "The Nature Theatre of Oklahoma" was always meant to be the final chapter. Kafka, says Brod, wanted the novel to end on a note of reconciliation. Brod admits that there are some gaps in the narrative immediately preceding this chapter, but he does not explain why he has omitted from the English edition two large extant fragments which are obviously part of the penultimate chapter. They appear only in the German edition.

There are reasonable grounds for supposing that Brod may have been led, by his desire to recreate Kafka in his own image, into misunderstanding the construction of *America*. A close examination reveals that the time-scale of the first seven chapters is such that the events related in them take place over a period of about four months. There is a lapse of approximately the same amount of time before the eighth chapter, "The Nature Theatre of Oklahoma," which also refers to events which have occurred during this missing period of time. For that matter, it also refers to the future in a way which makes

[14] *A*, p. 311.

it likely that Karl was to undergo further adventures. Kafka himself, in his Diaries, notes that the protagonists of *The Trial* and *America* are both to be killed: "Rossmann and K., the innocent and the guilty, both executed without distinction in the end, the guilty one with a gentler hand, more pushed aside than struck down."[15]

It is likely, therefore, that, in addition to the material missing from the English edition, there are large gaps in the narrative before the "Nature Theatre" chapter, and that it was not by any means intended as the conclusion of the novel. Charles Neider supports this contention to a great extent. His theory is that the first six chapters of *America* consist of two sections, each of three chapters, and that the plan of the book suggests a third section of three chapters. Chapters one to three portray what he calls "the narcissistic or homosexual factor in Karl's education." Chapters four to six "the platonic in terms of both male and female." The final three chapters, seven to nine, dealing with "the heterosexual factor in Karl's education" should, says Neider, consist of the chapters we are about to consider, separated by another chapter incorporating the two untranslated German fragments.[16] This seeems feasible, though one's reaction on reading the novel through very quickly in order to grasp its shape is that the "Nature Theatre of Oklahoma" reads better as a climax than as a conclusion.

Chapter VII, "A Refuge," describes Karl's first day and night with Delamarche, Robinson and Brunelda, the fat woman with whom Delamarche is living. Robinson has been forced to act as their servant, and it was because he was unable to cope with his many duties that he had been sent to fetch Karl. As Karl, after an unpleasant skirmish with a policeman, is allowing himself to be led upstairs to Brunelda's flat by Delamarche and Robinson, he notices three women, one of them a young

[15] *DFK*, Vol. 2, p. 132.
[16] Charles Neider: *Kafka, His Mind and Art*.

girl, who have come out into the corridor from a neigh-bouring apartment. Delamarche tries to stop him from looking at them:

> "These are disgusting women," said Delamarche, lowering his voice, it was evident, only out of con-sideration for the sleeping Brunelda, "sooner or later I'll report them to the police and then I'll be rid of them for years. Don't look their way," he snapped at Karl. But Karl had not seen any harm in looking at the women, since in any case he had to stand in the passage waiting for Brunelda to waken. And he shook his head angrily, as if he refused to take any admoni-tions from Delamarche, and he had just begun walking towards the women to make his meaning clearer, when Robinson caught him by the sleeve with the words: "Rossmann, take care!" while Delamarche, already exasperated, was roused to such fury by a loud burst of laughter from the girl that whirling his arms and legs he made a great spring at the women, who vanished into their doors as if they had been blown away.[17]

This is the first time that Karl has actively acknow-ledged any woman. The Manageress and Therese at the Hotel Occidental, and Pullunder's daughter Clara all had to take an aggressive role in their relations with him. His passive and indeed comparatively placid acceptance of them was indicative more of disinterest than of com-plaisance. But now, in refusing to be told by Delamarche that he must not look at the three women, he is beginning to act like a heterosexual male.

During the evening an election meeting takes place in the street outside, and is watched from the balcony by Brunelda and the three men. The election candidate is unable to make himself heard in the crowd. He acts out his meaningless charade, while on the balcony above

[17] *A*, pp. 234-5.

Karl does what his Uncle Jacob had warned him against: he gazes in helpless fascination at this curious segment of American life. Later in the evening, he manages to make contact with a young man who is reading on a neighbouring balcony. He is a shop worker by day who studies all night. But his study of medicine, it transpires, is senseless, it will lead him nowhere:

> ... I've studied for years now simply for the sake of mere consistency. I get very little satisfaction out of it and even less hope for the future. What prospects could I have? America is full of quack doctors.[18]

In other words, the student's actions have as little effect as those of the election candidate. If they have value, it is for him alone, and he is resigned to it. Karl, however, is not without hope for himself. He postpones his plan of immediate escape, and goes to sleep dreaming of a future.

The two untranslated fragments not available in the English edition belong here, before the "Nature Theatre" chapter. The first of them follows immediately upon the events of Chapter VII, and begins with Karl's awakening the following morning. He and Robinson prepare breakfast while Delamarche bathes Brunelda whose behaviour, as always, is that of an expressionist Brünnhilde. Karl is milder than he had been the previous evening, and makes attempts to please. Perhaps he has already forgotten that he meant to escape.

In the other fragment Robinson and Delamarche do not appear. Karl is looking after a chastened Brunelda. With the aid of the student he gets her into the street in an invalid's chair and wheels her along to a kind of brothel where apparently he will live with her. There is obviously a considerable gap in the narrative here, for by the beginning of the eighth chapter, "The Nature Theatre of Oklahoma," Karl is wandering aimlessly

[18] *A*, p. 279.

again, and is looking at a placard on a street corner.

The poster announces that people are being engaged for the giant Nature Theatre of Oklahoma. Everyone is welcome, everyone will be engaged. (Echoes of "Give me your poor . . ."?) But they must apply today: opportunity will not knock again. Karl goes to the race-course where recruiting is in progress and where he meets people he had known in earlier jobs. (There are several references here to episodes that are missing.) He is overwhelmed by the scale of the organisation:

> Before the entrance to the racecourse a long low platform had been set up, on which hundreds of women dressed as angels in white robes with great wings on their shoulders were blowing on long trumpets that glittered like gold. They were not actually stand-ing on the platform, but were mounted on separate pedestals, which could not however be seen, since they were completely hidden by the long flowing draperies of the robes. Now, as the pedestals were very high, some of them quite six feet high, these women looked gigantic, except that the smallness of their heads spoiled a little the impression of size, and their loose hair looked too short and almost absurd hanging between the great wings and framing their faces.[19]

Karl hastens to join up with this vast, odd theatre-circus. When we leave him, he is in the theatre-train on the long journey across America to Oklahoma. All those angels in billowy costumes blowing trumpets have pro-vided a marvellous welcome for Karl into the great broadstream of heterosexuality at last. As Neider points out, the recruiting women were costumed as angels whereas the men ("the cause of Karl's downfall")[20] who take over from them every two hours are dressed as devils.

But this is not really the end. Travelling on the

[19] *A*, p. 286.   [20] Neider, p. 100.

theatre-train with Karl is another recruit, an Italian boy Giacomo, who was one of the lift-boys at the Hotel Occidental.

For two days and nights they journeyed on. Only now did Karl understand how huge America was. Unweariedly he gazed out of the window, and Giacomo persisted in struggling for a place beside him until the other occupants of the compartment, who wanted to play cards, got tired of him and voluntarily surrendered the other window-seat. Karl thanked them—Giacomo's English was not easy for anyone to follow—and in the course of time, as is inevitable among fellow-travellers, they grew much more friendly, although their friendliness was sometimes a nuisance, as for example whenever they ducked down to rescue a card fallen on the floor, they could not resist giving hearty tweaks to Karl's legs or Giacomo's. Whenever that happened Giacomo always shrieked in renewed surprise and drew his legs up; Karl attempted once to give a kick in return, but suffered the rest of the time in silence.[21]

Karl travels on his possibly still ambiguous way, drawn into a future he cannot envisage. Whether he has, in fact, been developing from adolescent homosexuality to a more heterodox adult sexuality, is doubtful. Certainly he has not developed significantly in any other way. He remains picaresque and static: he collects and stores experience, but he has not learned how to sift it, how to make use of it. He has some distance along the road of pain and despair to travel before he grows into the K. of the later novels.

[21] *A*, p. 309.

CHAPTER V

THE TRIAL

As with Kafka's other two novels, a certain degree of uncertainty exists over the textual arrangement and, indeed, over the amount of text. All three novels are incomplete in their published versions; in the case of *The Trial* there is argument over just how much is missing. In an Epilogue to his version, Max Brod writes:

> For the division into chapters as well as the chapter headings Kafka is responsible, but for the arrangement of the chapters I have had to depend on my own judgment. Since, however, my friend had read me a great part of the manuscript, my judgment has been supported by actual recollection.
>
> Franz Kafka regarded the novel as unfinished. Before the final chapter, which is here included, various further stages of the mysterious trial should have been described. But since the trial, according to the author himself, was never to get as far as the highest Court, in a certain sense the novel was interminable; that is to say, it could be prolonged into infinity. And the finished chapters, taken in conjunction with the conclusive last chapter, in any case suffice to let the meaning and form of the work appear with the utmost clarity; anyone who was not informed that the author had proposed to do further work on it—he never did so, because his life entered an entirely new atmosphere—would scarcely notice its deficiencies.[1]

What Brod did, in effect, was to hold back from

[1] *T*, pp. 297-8.

publication any chapter which seemed to him obviously unfinished. He has made no textual alteration to what he has allowed to be published, but has worked out a chronology of his own in order to establish a chapter-order. In doing this, he has almost certainly indulged in an act of wilful "interpretation." Herman Uyttersprot[2] has proved that Brod's sequence is wrong, in an argument which, briefly, runs thus: *The Trial* is the only one of the novels whose chapter-sequence was not determined by the author himself. In the others, a strictly chronological order of events is followed, and there is no reason to imagine that Kafka would have departed from this in *The Trial*. Rearranging the chapters chronologically, one would arrive at the sequence 1, 4, 2, 3, 5, 6, 9, 7, 8 (followed by a considerable gap), 10. Uyttersprot further argues that about half of the novel is missing, just before the final chapter. This, however, is debatable.

In considering *The Trial*, therefore, although one had best follow the chapter sequence as published, one is well advised to refrain from basing any assertions, as many Kafka commentators have done, on the modern, dislocated time-sequence of the novel.

There is little point, at this stage in time, in pointing out that the English title, *The Trial*, chosen presumably by its translators Willa and Edwin Muir, is inaccurate. The German title, *Der Prozess*, really means "the law-suit" or "the legal procedure." (The word for trial is "Verhandlung.") But although the novel will no doubt always be known in English as *The Trial*, it ought to be remembered that *Prozess* is not only the legal word for law-suit, but also the German medical term for tuberculosis. Kafka was not suffering from TB when he wrote *The Trial*, or at any rate was not aware that he was, but if what he really was writing about was the attack of a killing disease, he may well have unconsciously called it

2 In an essay, "Zur Struktur von Kafka's *Der Prozess*. Versuch einer Neuordnung" (Brussels 1953). Collected in *Praags Cachet* (1963).

into existence, as Mahler did with his *Kindertotenlieder* which was followed by the death of his own child.

The Trial's opening sentence is one of those classically arresting ones: "Someone must have been telling lies about Joseph K., for without having done anything wrong he was arrested one fine morning."[3] With this matter-of-fact yet curiously resonant piece of information, a huge, exhausting and tragic parable of the human condition is set in motion, which can have only one outcome. Whether one understands it as the gnawing away of a fatal disease, or as neurosis worsening into self-destructive psychosis, or as man struggling with his original sin, its poetic and emotional meaning is unaffected. What it says may well be conveyed in different ways by different words, but meaning lies beyond words, and the meaning of Kafka's profound and gloomy creation is irrefutable.

Despite the nightmarish unreality of the events described, the style of *The Trial* is one of painstakingly detailed realism. Joseph K., a bank clerk, is arrested on the morning of his thirtieth birthday. The two policemen, or warders or whatever they are—their costumes do not make it clear—cannot or will not tell him why he has been arrested. Their job is simply to stand guard over him until the Inspector calls for him. Their job, one might say, is to make him doubt his innocence, his security, his assurance. They have arrested him in more ways than one. The nervous collapse is under way. Paralysis of the will has set in. At many points in the ensuing narrative, a healthy man would have been able to extricate and to free himself. A healthy man would not have complied with his

---

[3] *T*, p. 7 The references are to the page numbers of the latest reprinting of the Definitive Edition in which the Muirs' translation has been revised by Professor E. M. Butler. But the quotations are from the original translation which, where it differs from the revision, is to be preferred.

persecutors, would not have questioned himself. But then these things would never have happened to a healthy man. Joseph K. was healthy until they began to happen to him: but he must have borne within himself the conditions under which persecution could operate.

K. is interviewed by the Inspector in the room next door to his own, which is normally occupied by a Fräulein Bürstner. Later, he is allowed to go to his bank. He is merely under arrest, he is not yet to be taken into custody. And that same evening he waits up for Fräulein Bürstner so that he can apologise to her for her room having been used. For reasons he does not himself understand, he tries to make love to her. Is he attempting to establish his innocence by this futile sexual attack? Can it be that he is arrested in his sexual development, that at the age of thirty he has not grown up sexually, and that the trial he is about to undergo is connected with this? Perhaps K. wants quickly to prove, with the help of Fräulein Bürstner, that he is sexually adult, that the charge against him is groundless. If that is so, he does not succeed. His own introspection has begun a process of self-appraisal and self-condemnation, and he is powerless to stop it.

The following weekend, K. is summoned to a preliminary enquiry concerning his case. He has great difficulty in finding the court-room, in a house in the suburbs. Knocking on the doors of several rooms, he pretends he is looking for "a joiner called Lanz."[4] Eventually he asks his question of a young woman in a fifth-floor room washing children's clothes in a tub, and she gestures him through to an inner room:

K. felt as though he were entering a meeting-hall. A crowd of the most variegated people—nobody troubled about the newcomer—filled a medium-sized two-windowed room, which just below the roof was surrounded by a gallery, also quite packed, where the

[4] *T*, p. 45.

people were able to stand only in a bent posture with their heads and backs knocking against the ceiling. K., feeling the air too thick for him, stepped out again and said to the young woman, who seemed to have taken him up wrongly: "I asked for a joiner, a man called Lanz." "I know," said the woman, "just go right in." K. might not have obeyed if she had not come up to him, grasped the handle of the door, and said: "I must shut this door after you, nobody else must come in." "Very sensible," said K., "but the room is surely too full already." However, he went in again.[5]

It is only by accident that he has located the court; by accident or by instinct. The court itself is part of the instinctive process and has no independent existence. K. addresses it, delivering himself of a long, accusing harangue. He had been addressed by them as a house-painter, but the fact that he was not a house-painter seemed irrelevant to the court. Their indifference to him goads K. into a long and sarcastic speech. But it has no effect on the huge assemblage of officials. K.'s words have been no more than a vain and temporary solace to himself. On one level, he is enjoying the trial: he is a figure of some importance to these proceedings, whereas at his bank he is a somewhat insignificant clerk. His speech is interrupted by loud squeals from the back of the court-room, where one of the officials in a sudden attack of randiness has grabbed the woman who had earlier directed K. from her washing-tub in the outer room. This sensual outburst pricks the vanity of his speech as though it were a toy balloon.

By now, K. is deeply involved in the legal process. Although he receives no summons for the following Sunday, he makes his way to the court in any case, and finds no one there but the washerwoman who had been responsible for the disturbance the previous week. She

[5] *T*, pp. 46-47.

explains that her husband is the Law-Court Attendant, and she allows K. to look at the "law books" in the empty court. The first two he looks at turn out to be pornography and cheap fiction. The woman offers to help him; she has influence over the Examining Magistrate who is attracted to her. Their talk is interrupted now by a law student who eventually carries the woman off to the Examining Magistrate. The Law-Court Attendant appears and takes K. on a tour of the court's offices where, in a waiting room, he meets several other accused men.

K.'s attempt at some form of relationship with the washerwoman, intended to bolster his flagging self-respect, is an abject failure. The red-bearded, bandy-legged law student is able to carry her off without a struggle, and K. is left feeling worse than before. Again, in his own eyes, he becomes nothing more than someone or something accused. Although he continues to attempt some control of his actions, he has already lost. When he is shown round the court's offices, K. finds the atmosphere so stifling that he faints, and has to be helped outside. In the outside world, the world of the bank and of daily business, he feels well, the air he breathes does not sicken him, the future is always a possibility. But his values are overthrown by the court, he loses control over his mind and his body. The rules are different and he will never know them: he is a fish out of water, a man out of his proper element. Even the Clerk of Enquiries whom he meets and who actually helps him to leave the premises is a deeply disturbing figure in that he is unable to acknowledge the seriousness of speech. He is said to mean well, but in truth he means nothing. Nevertheless, K. needs his help. He is caught in the atmosphere of the court's offices as in a dream, and when the possibility of awakening occurs he is unable to avail himself of it without assistance. Even within the dream world of the trial, K. behaves as though he were neurotically in the grip of a dream within the dream. And, although momentarily he is thrust from the court's offices and out into the real world, he is already losing his grip on that outer reality. His gaze is increasingly an introspective one. If only he could, with sufficient vehemence or love, *see* something in the external world, something outside his own condition, it is possible that he would be saved. But the chances that he will even look meaningfully enough at the world around him are lessening day by day. Already he is guiltier, or less innocent, than when he was arrested.

In the chapter which follows in Brod's arrangement (IV, "Fräulein Bürstner's Friend"), K. finds a crippled girl, Fräulein Montag, moving in to share Fräulein Bürstner's room. She conveys a message to K. from Fräulein Bürstner refusing him an interview he had asked for. The landlady's nephew, Captain Lanz, is also involved with Fräulein Montag in some way. It does seem that this chapter ought to be placed earlier in the work, after Chapter I. For one thing, it would in that position lend some slight motivation to K.'s inventing "a joiner named Lanz" when he is looking for the court in Chapter II. True, he has heard of Captain Lanz in Chapter I, but only just. Besides, the opening sentence of Chapter IV, "In the next few days K. found it impossible to exchange even a word with Fräulein Bürstner,"[6] and the landlady's conversation later in the chapter suggest that it follows on from Chapter I. In its present position, it disturbs the onward rush, slackens the tension, and feels psychologically awkward.

What K. had hoped to gain from Fräulein Bürstner is not clear. Not sexual comfort, not confirmation of his lack of guilt. Simply, perhaps, some kind of help towards recognising a reality other than his own, which is by now considerably tarnished. His behaviour, in the comparative security of his own lodgings, is much firmer, less

[6] *T*, p. 86.

conciliatory than it is elsewhere. It is as though he felt that by asserting himself in his domestic surroundings he was somehow building up a wall of resistance to the shadowy world of the law-court which seemed only to exist, but then very forcibly, at weekends.

The fifth chapter, "The Whipper," is not one whose position is challenged by Uyttersprot. It is, however, disputed by Neider with, one feels, good reason. His contention is that it should precede Chapter III, "In the Empty Interrogation Chamber" where it would more effectively motivate K.'s sudden brutality towards one of the other accused whom he meets on his tour. His action could then be seen as being under the influence of the sadism of "The Whipper" episode. In addition, his neurotic reaction to the empty court-room could be understood in the light of the knowledge he would then have of the court's secret viciousness.

In "The Whipper," K. is about to leave his bank one evening when he hears groans from behind a door which he had always imagined to be the door of a store-room. He looks in, and sees three men, stooping somewhat because of the low ceiling:

> One of the men, who was clearly in authority over the other two and took the eye first, was sheathed in a sort of dark leather garment which left his throat and a good deal of his chest and the whole of his arms bare. He made no answer. But the other two cried: "Sir! We're to be flogged because you complained about us to the Examining Magistrate." And only then did K. realise that it was actually the warders Franz and Willem, and that the third man was holding a rod in his hand with which to beat them. "Why," said K., staring at them, "I never complained, I only told what happened in my rooms. And, anyhow, your behaviour there was not exactly blameless."[7]

[7] *T*, pp. 95-96.

K. is appalled, and attempts in vain to bribe the
Whipper to let them off. As the first strokes fall across
the back of the younger warder, he screams, and K.
rushes out into the corridor in embarrassment, afraid
that some of the bank staff will hear. He looks in the
store-room the following evening as he is about to leave
the bank, and to his horror the scene is as it was before,
about to start all over again. This time he shuts the door
in great haste, and angrily orders his junior clerks to
have the store-room cleared out as soon as possible.

The Whipper episode is the first intimation K. has
had of the sadistic physical violence that the court
apparently indulges in. When K. tells the Whipper that
he would never have complained about the warders had
he known they would be punished, he is told that that
makes no difference. They would have been punished in
any case. But really it is K. himself who wants to punish
the warders, who is ready to experience the same
sadistic fantasy over and over again.

Hitherto, the world of the law court had not infringed
upon K.'s day-to-day world of the bank. There were two
different spheres of influence, two completely separate
layers of consciousness. But now, behind a harmless
store-room door in the bank, the court has set up its
punishment chamber. K.'s condition is deteriorating.
The threat of the court is eating into his ordered daily
world. Simply by opening a door, he finds his safe and
solid reality is nothing more than a thin veneer. The
image of the whipping chamber is now terrifyingly close
to his consciousness. The remaining shreds of his
innocence are rapidly being stripped from him.

K.'s bribe fails, just as good works in the daytime
world fail, because they are motivated by guilt or fear.
The human condition cannot be improved, it can only
be suffered. Nor is there anything ennobling in human
endurance: man has no choice. Whatever is, is just.

K.'s uncle who lives in the country has heard about the

case and comes to town, ostensibly to assist his nephew. He has an old friend, an Advocate who might be able to help, so K. is taken to call on him. The Advocate, who is ill, astonishes K. by revealing that he already knows something of the affair. He has with him another visitor who turns out to be the Chief Clerk of the Court. But K. disgraces himself by leaving the room to search out the Advocate's nurse, Leni, and flirt with her.

The uncle's concern is really less with K.'s fortunes than with the possibility of family scandal. The Advocate's interest is a purely professional one. It is through him that the hitherto haphazard actions of the court are taken in hand and turned into something resembling a real legal trial, albeit a secret one. K., on the other hand, simply widens and diversifies his various areas of guilt, by becoming involved with Leni. He runs the risk of forfeiting the tenuous good-will of the three old men who are talking about him in another room. But he is incapable of acting differently. In his attempt to prove himself a free agent, he merely hastens the determined outcome.

Leni attempts to make K. renounce his fiancée Elsa, of whom we know very little in any case. He carries a photograph of Elsa, but neither shows any great concern for her nor appears to expect any in return. When K. kisses Leni, she exclaims: "You have exchanged her for me."[8] Perhaps he has: none of his relationships with women who vaguely offer to help him last very long. But Leni gives him the key to her door, and tells him he can come whenever he wants to. When he leaves the house, he finds his uncle impatiently waiting in his car:

"Boy!" he cried, "How could you do it! You have terribly damaged your case, which was beginning to go quite well. You hide yourself away with a filthy little trollop, who is obviously the Advocate's mistress

[8] *T*, p. 125.

into the bargain, and stay away for hours. You don't even seek any pretext, you conceal nothing, no, you're quite open, you simply run off to her and stay beside her. And all this time we three sit there, your uncle, who is doing his best for you, the Advocate, who has to be won over to your side, above all the Chief Clerk of the Court, a man of importance, who is actually in charge of your case at its present stage. There we sit, consulting how to help you, I have to handle the Advocate circumspectly, and the Advocate in turn the Clerk of the Court, and one might think you had every reason to give me at least some support. Instead of which you absent yourself. You were away so long that there was no concealing it; of course the two gentlemen, being men of the world, didn't talk about it, they spared my feelings, but finally even they couldn't get over it, and as they couldn't mention it they said nothing at all."[9]

K. is by now so immersed in his psychosis that he apparently does not even reply to his uncle's angry words. If innocence is health, he is by now riddled with guilt. Nevertheless, he is still capable of fighting; he has by no means abandoned the idea of innocence. And he accepts the services of the Advocate for what they are worth, visiting him for consultations and holding hands surreptitiously with Leni during tea.

Was the Advocate seeking to comfort him or to drive him to despair? K. could not tell, but he soon held it for an established fact that his defence was not in good hands. It might be all true, of course, what the Advocate said, though his attempts to magnify his own importance were transparent enough and it was likely that he had never till now conducted such an important case as he made K's out to be. But his continual bragging of his personal connexions with the

[9] *T*, pp. 125-6.

officials was suspicious. Was it so certain that he was
exploiting these connexions for K.'s benefit?[10]

The Advocate's advice is virtually meaningless, even
absurd. And his comfort is certainly cold. K. learns that
there is no recognised form of procedure in the court, that
its officials are corrupt, that there is no known way of
finding out the exact nature of the charge. Understandably, his work at the bank suffers. Faced with inter-
viewing a client, a manufacturer who has come to talk
about an overdraft or some such matter, he finds himself
neurotically unable to concentrate, or even to go
through the required motions of politely listening to the
man's proposals. When the Deputy Manager comes in
from his office next door and takes the manufacturer off
his hands, K. can react only by staring out of the window
in a state of agonised indecision. The manufacturer
comes through K.'s office again on his way out and,
noticing K.'s distracted behaviour, confides that he
knows something of K.'s case, and claims that he may be
able to help in some way. He is acquainted with a dis-
reputable character, a painter named Titorelli who
occasionally works for the court and who knows several
of the Judges, and he advises K. to get in touch with him.
This K. immediately proceeds to do, in a burst of manic
energy, abandoning his other bank appointments for the
afternoon, all of which are taken over by the Deputy
Manager.

Titorelli, who has painted several portraits of the
judges, is impressed by K.'s claim to be innocent, and
feels confident that he can get K. acquitted; not by
presenting evidence, or pleading a case, of course, but by
using his influence with the judges. But he confuses K.
by pointing out to him that there is more than one kind
of acquittal:

Titorelli drew his chair closer to the bed and con-

[10] *T*, p. 140.

tinued in a low voice: "I forgot to ask you first what sort of acquittal you want. There are three possibilities, that is, definite acquittal, ostensible acquittal, and indefinite postponement. Definite acquittal is of course the best, but I haven't the slightest influence on that kind of verdict. As far as I know, there is no single person who could influence the verdict of definite acquittal. The only deciding factor seems to be the innocence of the accused. Since you're innocent, of course it would be possible for you to ground your case on your innocence alone. But then you would require neither my help nor help from anyone."[11]

Definite acquittal has never been known. Ostensible acquittal and postponement, when explained, sound like the inventions of a very grim Lewis Carroll. One is not surprised that no definite acquittal exists: no man is completely innocent. Ostensible acquittal allows the defendent to continue to live his life under the constant threat of new arrest. This is the condition in which the vast majority of civilised mankind exists. Postponement allows one to come to terms eventually with the infinite, to defer payment of punishment in the temporal world.

K. determines to take his case out of the Advocate's hands, particularly after meeting a fellow-client of the Advocate, a commercial traveller named Block, whose life appears to have been ruined not so much by his case as by his complete and slavish dependence upon the Advocate. For Block, his trial has become the one thing he lives for. All else is subordinated to it, even the eventual verdict will seem irrelevant to him. Existence has come to be centred around the problem of his guilt: he has dwindled into becoming a religious fanatic. K. no doubt fears the same fate.

The chapter (VIII) in which K. decides to take his case out of the Advocate's hands ought surely to precede

[11] *T*, pp. 170-1.

Chapter VII in which he tries to enlist the painter's aid, rather in the mood of one who, told by respectable physicians that his case is hopeless, is reduced to seeking the advice of quacks and charlatans. But no Kafka commentator appears to have suggested a rearrangement of these two chapters.

It is obvious that K.'s case, and Kafka's narration of it, cannot continue in this strain indefinitely, though it is equally obvious that there can be very little possibility of further significant development. The process could continue endlessly; the end, when it comes, will be arbitrary. K. has already been driven to irrationality in his day-to-day behaviour: his situation is desperate, and perhaps he now somewhere deep within himself begins to realise it. The novel, if one can venture the opinion without sounding flippant, has been almost as exhausting an experience for the reader as the events described in it have been for its protagonist. And so it ought to be. At the end of his emotional tether, K. gathers his resources for the final resolving of the situation. Where else can he turn now, reason having deserted him, but to God?

He has been given the job of showing one of the bank's Italian clients the art treasures in the cathedral. The Italian fails to turn up, and K. finds himself wandering about alone in the murky cathedral interior. The author's device to get him there may strike the reader at this point as being somewhat clumsy or, at the best, offhand. But it turns out to have been a device not of Kafka's but of the court's. In the otherwise empty cathedral K. finds a priest about to ascend into the pulpit. Is there to be a service, without congregation, without even music? He is about to leave when suddenly the priest's voice rings out through the gloom. It calls his own name: "Joseph K."[12]

The priest, who is also the prison chaplain, informs K. that he has been found guilty. He tells him a curious

[12] *T*, p. 234.

parable about a door-keeper who stands guard before
the Law, and then proceeds to discuss its interpretation
with K. This priest or chaplain has no comfort for K.
His concern, after all, is with God, and his viewpoint is
even more remote from K.'s than is that of the court. It
has taken K. some months to understand that, although,
in theory, innocence is an admissible concept in law, the
court which is dealing with him has never known an
innocent person, has certainly never admitted anyone to
be innocent.

There can, of course, be no question of the priest
accepting K.'s claim to be innocent. Such presumption is
merely a proof of guilt, if any proof were needed. In
fighting the court, K. has apparently been fighting the
appointed instrument of divine justice. What hope, then,
can there be for him? Poor K., with his book of tourist
views of the city which he clutches as most people in
church clutch a prayer-book, is beyond redemption.
The Law is everything, and it has washed its hands of K.

"Don't you want anything more to do with me?"
asked K. "No," said the priest. "You were so friendly
to me for a time," said K., "and explained so much to
me, and now you let me go as if you cared nothing
about me." "But you have to leave now," said the
priest. "Well, yes," said K., "you must see that I can't
help it." "You must first see that I can't help being
what I am," said the priest. "You are the prison
chaplain," said K., groping his way nearer to the
priest again; his immediate return to the Bank was not
so necessary as he had made out, he could quite well
stay longer. "That means I belong to the Court," said
the priest. "So why should I make any claims upon
you? The Court makes no claims upon you. It receives
you when you come and it relinquishes you when you
go."[13]

[13] *T*, p. 248.

There is no more to be said. One awaits the end. And
it comes when, on the evening before his thirty-first
birthday, exactly one year after his initial arrest, two
men arrive at K.'s lodgings. Although he has not been
told to expect them, K. is sitting quietly in an arm-chair,
dressed in black. He greets them with "So you are
appointed for me?"[14] The two frock-coated men remove
their top hats, and bow. Taking K. out into the street,
they grip his arms forcibly and march him off. K. has a
moment or two of hysterical humour. The melodramatic
appearance of the two men at first makes him mutter
"Tenth-rate old actors they send for me."[15] And, catching
sight of their double chins under a lamp-light, he
wonders if they could be operatic tenors. He tries to
resist them, but is impelled onwards. He thinks they pass
Fräulein Bürstner, or at least a woman who resembles
her. K.'s last thoughts as he is marched on are dulled,
lucid, timeless, resigned.

"The only thing I can do now," he told himself, and
the regular correspondence between his steps and the
steps of the other two confirmed his thought, "the only
thing for me to go on doing is to keep my intelligence
calm and discriminating to the end. I always wanted
to snatch at the world with twenty hands, and not for
a very laudable motive, either. That was wrong, and
am I to show now that not even a whole year's struggling with my case has taught me anything? Am I to
leave this world as a man who shies away from all
conclusions? Are people to say of me after I am gone
that at the beginning of my case I wanted it to finish,
and at the end of it wanted it to begin again? I don't
want that to be said. I am grateful for the fact that
these half-dumb, stupid creatures have been sent to
accompany me on this journey, and that I have been
left to say to myself all that is needed."[16]

[14] *T*, p. 249.   [15] *T*, p. 249.   [16] *T*, pp. 251-2.

K G

When they reach a deserted quarry outside the town, the two men remove K.'s coat, waistcoat and shirt. They lay him on the ground, his head on a rock, and, producing a double-edged butcher's knife, they make it clear that K. himself is expected to guide the knife into his breast. But this responsibility he silently insists on leaving to them. At the last moment a window somewhere is flung up. It is the last proud flicker of hope, and the knife is already turning in his heart. "Like a dog," murmurs K. as he dies.[17]

K. had spent a year searching for a possible and guiltless life, a meaningful life. He has found only a meaningless death in a quarry at the end of a butcher's knife. The tale told by an idiot, full of sound and fury, signifying nothing, is ended. He leaves behind him only the lingering shame of his death.

Either K. is Everyman or he is nobody; either *The Trial* is, as is almost everything that Kafka wrote, a parable of some aspect of the human condition, or it is a pretentious, meaningless and monstrous tale. In other words, either it strikes off deep and resonant responses within the reader, or it completely fails to affect him. That the story is open to more than one interpretation is undeniable, and is surely an indication of its universal validity. Different temperaments respond differently to it. It can even vary its meaning to any one reader at different times. *The Trial* is, in short, a valid aesthetic experience, but it is valid only by virtue of being something more. To call it, as well one might, a psychological masochistic fantasy is by no means to relegate it to an inferior or invalid category. Some of our most profound modern insights have come to us from areas of apparent mental sickness. To discuss *The Trial* in Freudian terms is to describe its genesis rather than its nature. It exists not as part of the casebook of Franz Kafka but as a work of art, and a deeply meaningful one. The "Prozess" may

[17] *T*, p. 255.

be tuberculosis, the trial may be a religious experience or a nervous crisis. It may be the development of a personality that is under arrest. The pattern has its own meaning. Form unites, content divides. In its formal unity, *The Trial*, incomplete though it is, is a unique and disturbing vision of the kind of hell to which we, or our judges within us, condemn ourselves.

Kafka himself at one time thought of *The Trial* as a parable of the individual and responsibility. It is a reasonable interpretation: some are called to adulthood by nervous crises, particularly if their adolescent life has been thoughtlessly and superficially experienced. It is the kind of crisis that sometimes comes to a man when he is thirty. Kafka has externalised these nameless fears in *The Trial*: he has given them, with almost Shakespearian precision, a local habitation and a name.

CHAPTER VI

THE CASTLE

It could almost be said that Kafka did not write three novels, but wrote or attempted to write one novel three times. It is certainly true that in all three books he continues to gnaw away at variations on the same theme. His three concerti for man and society may differ in detail, but in all of them the apparent concern is with man's attempt to integrate himself into the company of his fellow-men. Karl Rossmann in *America* thought to do it by being successful, Joseph K. in *The Trial* by establishing his innocence. K., as again he is called, in *The Castle*, the last of the three novels and probably Kafka's most complex and significant work, wants desperately to belong, to be domiciled.

Again, the novel is unfinished. Kafka's compulsive inability to bring any of his longer works to a conclusion ~r failed him. And, as with the other novels, we have Kafka's expressed intention that it should end with the death of the "K" figure. In an Editor's Note, Max Brod writes:

Kafka never wrote the concluding chapter. But he told me about it once when I asked him how the novel was to end. The ostensible Land Surveyor was to find partial satisfaction at least. He was not to relax in his struggle, but was to die worn out by it. Round his death-bed the villagers were to assemble, and from the Castle itself the word was to come that though K.'s legal claim to live in the village was not valid, yet, taking certain auxiliary circumstances into account, he was to be permitted to live and work there.[1]

As always, Kafka wastes neither time nor words in beginning his narrative. *The Castle* starts with K.'s arrival, late one winter evening, at a small, snow-covered village whose houses huddle around a castle on top of a hill. He finds the village inn still open, is told there are no rooms available but that he can sleep in a corner of the parlour. While several villagers are still drinking, he lies down and falls asleep, only to be awakened by a young man who tells him that unless he has permission from the Count up at the Castle, he cannot pass the night in the village. K. claims to be a Land Surveyor whom the Count is expecting, and a telephone call is put through to the Castle to confirm this. At first it seems that the Castle has denied all knowledge of a Land Surveyor, but the phone rings a second time: K. is expected, all is in order. This appears to disturb K.:

> So the Castle had recognised him as the Land Surveyor. That was unpropitious for him, on the one hand, for it meant that the Castle was well informed about him, had estimated all the probable chances, and was taking up the challenge with a smile. On the other hand, however, it was quite propitious, for if his interpretation were right they had underestimated his strength, and he would have more freedom of action than he had dared to hope. And if they expected to cow him by their lofty superiority in recognising him as Land Surveyor, they were mistaken; it made his skin prickle a little, that was all.[2]

We are plunged into these events in the first pages of *The Castle*. What are we to make of K.'s reaction to the Castle's afterthought concerning him? Are we meant to believe that he is really a Land Surveyor? This is

[1] *C*, p. 8.   [2] *C*, p. 15.

extremely doubtful. His first drowsy words to the young
man who awakens him in the name of the Castle, are
"What village is this I have wandered into? Is there a
castle here?"[3] And his disquiet at eventually having his
story accepted by the Castle authorities at the other end
of the phone is that of a trickster whose bluff has been
called.

If K. is a trickster in any sense, he is no ordinary one.
But his identity can, should, be questioned. Perhaps his
winter journey, like that of Müller's *Winterreise* wayfarer,
is a search for identity, and for acceptance, which may
well be the same thing. Why should the Castle's recognition of K. as the Land Surveyor he claims to be make his
skin prickle? As we progress into the maze of the narrative we shall find ourelves sympathising with K. in his
vain quest, but we ought not to lose sight of our own
initial doubts about him. *The Castle* is, amongst other
things, a study of relationships, of individual to society,
of ego to id, of thought to action, of sickness to health,
perhaps of Jew to Gentile. Joseph K., the passive victim
of *The Trial*, has become K., the aggressive protagonist of
The Castle. He has nothing to fear from the Castle but
non-recognition of his identity. The day after his un-
propitious arrival, K. explores the village and meets
some of the villagers including the schoolmaster. They
are neither hostile nor friendly. He finds a man with a
sledge who refuses to take him to the Castle, but brings
him back to the inn. Here K. finds that the Castle has
sent him two assistants, and soon he acquires a third, a
messenger from the Castle, called Barnabas, But a phone
call to the Castle to ask when he will be allowed to call
there elicits the response: "Never."[4]

K. continues to scheme and plot, and through Barnabas and his family he becomes acquainted with another
inn, the Herrenhof, where some of the Castle officials
sometimes stay. One of the officials, Klamm, appears

[3] *C*, p. 12.   [4] *C*, p. 35.

to be in charge of K.'s case, but K. is unable to contact him. He spends a night at the Herrenhof on the bar-room floor amid the beer puddles, making love to the barmaid, Frieda, who is Klamm's mistress. After shouting through the door of Klamm's room that she is now with the Land Surveyor, Frieda accompanies him back to the other inn and moves into the small room that K. is already sharing with his assistants. Frieda is neither young nor pretty, yet K. continues his compulsive sexual sessions with her:

"I believe I know what you mean," she said, and she clung to his neck and tried to say something else but could not go on speaking, and since their chair was close to it they reeled over and fell on the bed. There they lay, but not in the forgetfulness of the previous night. She was seeking and he was seeking, they raged and contorted their faces and bored their heads into each other's bosoms in the urgency of seeking some-thing, and their embraces and their tossing limbs did not avail to make them forget, but only reminded them of what they sought; like dogs desperately tearing up the ground they tore at each other's bodies, and often, helplessly baffled, in a final effort to attain happiness they nuzzled and tongued each other's face. Sheer weariness stilled them at last and brought them gratitude to each other. Then the maids came in. "Look how they're lying there," said one, and sympathetically cast a coverlet over them.[5]

The landlady of the inn, a kind of crypto-mother to Frieda, concerns herself with the relationship. She is scornful of K. who by now is determined to see Klamm not only with reference to his gaining access to the Castle, but also in order to receive Klamm's permission for him to marry Frieda. To be accepted is what K. really needs. Presumably he could, when he first arrived in the village,

[5] C, pp. 63-64.

have walked up to the Castle and knocked on the door.
If he accepts the myth of its impregnability, its strange
power, it can only be because his real desires are more
complex than he imagines them to be. To force his way
into the Castle as a stranger is not K.'s purpose. To be
accepted, to be recognised, to be given a part to play is
vitally necessary to him. This is why he continues to
grapple his way to the Castle, accepting involvement at
every turn. The other way would be the lonely way from
which he is desperately trying to escape.

The maze of involvement becomes more complex.
K. manages, without too much difficulty, to obtain an
interview with a comparatively lowly official, the Mayor
of the village or, as he is known in the Edwin and Willa
Muir translation, the Superintendent, a kindly man who
suffers from gout. The Mayor informs K., somewhat
cryptically, that he has been taken on as Land Surveyor,
but that unfortunately the village has no need of a
surveyor as everything has already been surveyed and
recorded. He tells K. something of the complicated
bureaucratic detail involved in the administration of the
village.

K.'s hopeless fight for recognition now begins to be
seen as a struggle to come to grips with reality. The
reality of the Castle is surrounded, rendered almost
unattainable, by the confusion of life in the village. The
Mayor sows doubts in K.'s mind as to the reality of
events which hitherto K. has taken for granted. The
telephone messages from the Castle may or may not
have been real, but are almost certainly insignificant to
the point of meaninglessness, due to the confusion of the
telephone system and to the fact that there is no central
exchange. The only reality is the Castle itself. K. has
infiltrated himself sufficiently into the workings of the
bureaucratic machine for there no longer to be any
question of his being forced to leave. But he can get no
further forward: he can still not penetrate to the inner

reality. He differs from the villagers primarily in that they are not interested in defining their relationship to the Castle. They are aware of its existence, perhaps even slightly fearful of it, but it does not influence their daily life in the slightest degree. K., on the other hand, never loses sight of it. All else is subordinated to his image of the Castle as the ultimate authority: truth, reality, the inner life, or perhaps simply the goal of life. He has no option but to persevere.

The landlady confides in K. that twenty years ago she too had been Klamm's mistress. In fact, it seems usual for the village women to give themselves to the Castle officials: this is the only kind of contact that exists between Castle and village. Castle and village, then, are male and female. The passive feminine principle is now being undermined by K. who, non-conformist, refuses to adopt a passive attitude towards the male Castle. K. is a lonelier, more adult being than the Joseph K. of *The Trial* who wanted simply to be restored to his condition of pristine innocence. K. has an almost Promethean determination, but with it and within him is coupled that Jewish quasi-masochism that is a characteristic of all Kafka's protagonists. He must act as he does, and we see now that he is no superficial impostor as we feared he might be at the beginning, but an earnest seeker after truth and reality who is willing to use the subterfuges of the world in order to go on living in the world. At the instigation of the Mayor, the village schoolmaster offers K. the temporary position of school janitor. K.'s first impulse is to indignantly refuse the offer, but Frieda persuades him to accept. It is, after all, temporary, and it is recognition of a kind. But before taking up his duties, K. pays another visit to the Herrenhof. As he walks along the snowbound village streets, he looks up at the dark, silent Castle.

The Castle, whose contours were already beginning

to dissolve, lay silent as ever; never yet had K. seen
there the slightest sign of life—perhaps it was quite
impossible to recognise anything at that distance, and
yet the eye demanded it and could not endure that
stillness. When K. looked at the Castle, often it seemed
to him as if he were observing someone who sat quietly
there in front of him gazing, not lost in thought and
so oblivious of everything, but free and untroubled, as
if he were alone with nobody to observe him, and yet
must notice that he was observed, and all the same
remained with his calm not even slightly disturbed;
and really—one did not know whether it was cause or
effect—the gaze of the observer could not remain
concentrated there, but slid away. This impression
today was strengthened still further by the early dusk;
the longer he looked, the less he could make out and
the deeper everything was lost in the twilight.[6]

Thus is the Castle revealed as benevolent but un-
perturbed authority. K. looks at it as the young Kafka
once used to look at his father. Just as Franz needed to be
accepted, to be acknowledged by his remote parent, so
K. desires the approval of the Castle and its acceptance
of him as an important functionary in its service.

Arriving at the Herrenhof, K. meets a young girl,
Pepi, who is obviously Frieda's successor with Klamm.
He restrains himself from making advances to her,
although he is tempted to do so not so much by her
personal charms as by her statement that formerly she
had been a chambermaid at the Castle. Here is a direct
link with the Castle: not a very meaningful one, it is true,
but nevertheless a contact, however tenuous, with
reality. K. decides to wait for Klamm, but misses him
and instead is forced to undergo being interviewed by
Klamm's "village secretary," a young man called
Momus. At first, disappointed at having failed to meet

[6] *C*, pp. 126-7.

Klamm, K. tries to leave, but is momentarily brought up short by Momus's slamming a document down on the table and shouting "In the name of Klamm, I command you to answer my questions."[7] The landlady, who inexplicably has contrived to be present, tries to impress K. with the importance of Momus and the significance of being interviewed by him.

Consider [she says] that Klamm appointed him, that he acts in Klamm's name, that what he does, even if it never reaches Klamm, has yet Klamm's assent in advance. And how can anything have Klamm's assent that isn't filled by his spirit? Far be it from me to offer Herr Momus crude flattery—besides he would absolutely forbid it himself—but I'm speaking of him not as an independent person, but as he is when he has Klamm's assent, as at present; then he's an instrument in the hand of Klamm, and woe to anybody who doesn't obey him.[8]

Momus, then, is an important intermediary. The way to the Castle is through Klamm, the way to Klamm is through Momus. It would appear that at least K.'s efforts are being channelled in the right direction, and that he is making some kind of progress. Yet even this is illusory. Momus is village secretary not only to Klamm but also to another official, Vallabene. His significance is thus somewhat diffuse: he is a kind of crossroads which could as easily lead K. off in a wrong direction. He accepts a deposition from K. which he will place in Klamm's village register. But the importance of the village register is by no means clearly defined. As a repository of unconscious memory it may have some validity, but as a means of advancing K. towards the Castle it may be worse than useless.

K.'s belief in the Castle never wavers. Sidetracked though he may be by village secretaries, by temporary

[7] *C*, p. 142.   [8] *C*, p. 147.

jobs as school janitors, by his two absurd assistants or by Frieda, he is steadfast in his faith or in his search for faith. He has no sooner left the Herrenhof than he runs into his two assistants with Barnabas the messenger. It appears that the Castle is trifling with him, for Barnabas bears a letter from Klamm congratulating K. and his assistants on the surveying work he has carried out, and insisting that they should continue in their task without interruption. K., of course, is in no condition to appreciate the element of humour in such a letter, he is simply made weary by it. He tries to persuade Barnabas to take a message back to Klamm at the Castle immediately, but it transpires that Barnabas has not yet delivered his last message, that he is under no compulsion to deliver messages promptly, and that in any case Klamm hates receiving messages.

K. makes his way to the school where, as janitor, he is to sleep in one of the classrooms with Frieda and the two assistants. There are, naturally, no beds, only a sack of straw. They spend together a cold and miserable night which is enlivened only by one curious incident:

K. was awakened during the night by some noise or other, and in his first vague sleepy state felt for Frieda; he found that, instead of Frieda, one of the assistants was lying beside him. Probably because of the exacerbation which being suddenly awakened is sufficient in itself to cause, this gave him the greatest fright that he had ever had since he first came to the village. With a cry he sat up, and not knowing what he was doing he gave the assistant such a buffet that he began to cry. However the whole thing was cleared up in a moment. Frieda had been awakened—at least so it had seemed to her—by some huge animal, a cat probably, which had sprung on to her breast and then leapt away again. She had got up and was searching the whole room for the beast with a candle. One of the assistants had seized the opportunity to enjoy the sack of straw for a little, an attempt which he was now bitterly repenting. Frieda could find nothing, however; perhaps it had only been a delusion, she went back to K. and on the way she stroked the crouching and whimpering assistant over the hair to comfort him, as if she had forgotten the evening's conversation. K. said nothing, but he asked the assistant to stop putting wood on the fire, for owing to almost all the heap having been squandered the room was already too hot.[9]

K.'s predicament is, in its way, more desperate than Joseph K.'s in *The Trial*. The lawsuit was bound to end in a verdict of guilt, and punishment was sure to follow. Death is the end. It is by no means certain that K.'s quest in *The Castle* need cause his death. In fact, a difficulty of the work is that there can, really, be no end. Life is spent in striving for an unattainable goal. However much life is prolonged, the goal remains unattainable. Either one is born within the Castle, if indeed anyone at all inhabits it, or one's life is spent vainly attempting to gain entrance. Even the meaningless pursuits of career, such as becoming a school janitor, are indulged in as part of the campaign.

On the morning after their first night at the school, K. and Frieda awaken to find the pupils clustered around them. The woman teacher behaves hysterically, the schoolmaster himself arrives and sides with her, and an absurd scene develops in which K. is dismissed but refuses to accept dismissal. Frieda asks K. to take her away to the south of France or to Spain, but departure is something of which K. simply cannot conceive:

"I can't go away," replied K. "I came here to stay. I'll stay here." And giving utterance to a self-contradiction which he made no effort to explain, he added as if to himself: "What could have enticed me

[9] *C*, p. 161.

to this desolate country except the wish to stay here?"[10]

K. will not leave the village, but Frieda herself leaves
K. in order to look after one of the assistants whom K.
has chased away. The narrative becomes heavier, thicker
with incident. Barnabas and his family assume a greater
significance. One of his sisters, Amalia, had once
rejected a court official, as a result of which the family
have become social outcasts. The other sister Olga
prostitutes herself with the Castle officials at the Herrenhof in a vain attempt to restore the family fortunes. Olga
surprises K. by telling him that Klamm's actual appearance is variable. He can, apparently, present different
faces to different people:

"But we do often speak about Klamm, whom I've
never seen; you know Frieda doesn't like me and has
never let me look at him, still his appearance is well
known in the village, some people have seen him,
everybody has heard of him, and out of glimpses and
rumours and through various distorting factors an
image of Klamm has been constructed which is
certainly true in fundamentals. But only in fundamentals. In detail it fluctuates, and yet perhaps not so
much as Klamm's real appearance. For he's reported
as having one appearance when he comes into the
village and another on leaving it; after having his beer
he looks different from what he does before it, when
he's awake he's different from when he's asleep, when
he's alone he's different from when he's talking to
people, and—what is incomprehensible after all that
—he's almost another person up in the Castle. And
even within the village there are considerable differences in the accounts given of him, differences as to his
height, his bearing, his size, and the cut of his beard;
fortunately there's one thing in which all the accounts
agree, he always wears the same clothes, a black

[10] *C* p. 172.

morning coat with long tails. Now of course all these differences aren't the result of magic, but can be easily explained; they depend on the mood of the observer, on the degree of his excitement, on the countless graduations of hope or despair which are possible for him when he sees Klamm, and besides, he can usually see Klamm only for a second or two."[11]

It is even possible that Momus, Klamm's village secretary, is Klamm himself. But K. needs to be re-assured of Klamm's true existence: this man, whom he probably has not yet seen, is his only important link with the Castle. Doubt of any kind means disaster. Doubt, however, has been introduced. Doubt as to the very existence of Klamm. Doubt as to whether the end will ever be attained. This, to K., is a paralysing blow though he does not immediately realise it. From this moment, his grip on reality, which has at best been tenuous, begins to falter. A message delivered by Barnabas leads him to believe that one of Klamm's chief secretaries Erlanger has asked to see the Land Surveyor at the Herrenhof in room 15:

"But he must come at once. I've only a few things to settle there and I leave again for the Castle at five o'clock in the morning. Tell him that it's very im-portant that I should speak to him."[12]

When K. arrives at the Herrenhof, he finds a small group of applicants waiting for Erlanger. K. misses him and instead sees a Castle secretary named Bürgel who, in long, rambling and discursive fashion, tells K. how he can obtain admission to the Castle by unofficially accosting one of the secretaries by night when the official power of judgment suffers somewhat. K. un-fortunately is by this time too tired to understand Bürgel correctly. He does grasp, however, that he must

[11] *C*, pp. 216-7.   [12] *C*, p. 291.

by-pass the regulations in some way. And it is something of this that he tries to pass on to Pepi, Klamm's barmaid. Soon, the novel as Kafka wrote it trails to an end: K.'s dilemma is still acute. He is demanding by right an entry into a community whose laws and customs he has begun to despise. It is vital not only to his happiness but also to his very existence that he should attain his impossible goal. Brod has told us that K. was, ironically, to die just as the possibility, not of complete acceptance by the Castle, but of some form of *modus vivendi* was about to be granted him. To K. the Castle was the only reality. But the Castle was surely only another aspect of illusion, and it was precisely because it was illusion that it was unattainable. Happiness is illusory. And Kafka's own personality and temperament rendered it unlikely that he would be able to find any real equilibrium between village and Castle, between his Jewishness and the Austro-Hungarian world around him, between the bourgeois business-world of his father and his own private artist's life. "What could have enticed me into this desolate land but the desire to stay here?" It is the exile's question, and it is surely the saddest and most unanswerable question that K., or Kafka, could have asked.

By being brought to a condition where he could bear to question himself in this way, K. proves himself more pliable than Rossmann in *America*, more capable of being acted upon by the external world than Joseph K. in *The Trial* who, mentally unstable and impregnable, allowed only one thing to happen to him: a knife to be plunged into his breast. K. may never reach The Castle, but he has reached an advanced stage of self-discovery on the way, and to this extent he is less inflexibly ego-centric a character than his predecessors in the earlier two novels. He has stormed the Castle within himself. Does Kafka mean us to know this? One is not certain.

CHAPTER VII

CRITICS AND A CONCLUSION

Kafka's stature, as one of the four or five really first-rate novelists of the first half of our century, has to some extent, been assumed. He is a worthy peer of Proust, Mann, Svevo, Musil and Joyce. Kafka may lack the final consummate artistry of Mann, or the psychological acumen of Proust, but he has a unique validity as a novelist thrown up by the crisis in art and philosophy at the turn of the century. He is both symptom and product of his age, depicting with a frightening exactitude the dilemma of modern man in search of a soul. The nature of his art, the subject of his concern, is such that he has been widely and variously interpreted, as well as differently appraised, by an impressive array of critics. The Kafka literature in the forty or so years since his death has reached really vast proportions, and it would be impossible even to list it all here. It may, however, be useful to consider the two or three principal trends and the most interesting and articulate exponents of them, concentrating our attention on critical exegesis of the novels.

When Thomas Mann gave Albert Einstein a Kafka novel to read, Einstein handed it back to him after a few days, admitting that he had failed to finish it. "The human mind," said Einstein, "isn't that complex." Einstein, in other words, made the elementary mistake of imagining the creation of a work of art, whether novel, symphony or painting, to be an intellectual process. This, let it be spelled out, is not the way the artist functions. Einstein's critical mind was complex enough to have considered and understood the several meanings, if meanings one must find, in the novels of Kafka, but he chose to misunderstand the problem. One of Kafka's most perceptive and illuminating critics, Charles Neider, has, however, come to an understanding of the works through an intelligent and open-minded reading of them. The human mind is complex enough, if it allows itself to be. Neider's investigation of Kafka is conducted from both literary and psychological viewpoints. Examining the neuroses of the heroes of the three novels, he describes Karl Rossman as naively neurotic, Joseph K. as savagely neurotic, and K. as philosophically neurotic.

These three heroes, who are not heroic in the romantic sense, are the dangling young men of the modern novel. Their world is thin, with little furniture, most of it rotten. They are bewildered by the authority of specialisation and the crushing burden of accumulated facts. They resent the interim period in which they live and the remoteness of their fathers' world. They resent the collapse of faith visible all around them. They are unwilling to sublimate their personal neurosis in the collective neurosis of a shallow faith. Therefore they forge a profound neurosis of their own. They refuse to believe in the baseless simply because it is an anchor. On the other hand, they cannot find faith in disbelief. Therefore they dangle. They are not men of action. They possess no stage and their muscles are cramped, their bones mildewed. Worst of all, they lack the heart for action. Nor are they men of experience. Being deprived of myths, they are overwhelmed by the complexity and irrationality of nature; therefore they turn their backs on her, avert their eyes before beauty, shun truth as a plague except when verbalising it, dangling it with themselves. They are more interested in arguing "What is truth?" than in examining some of its causes and effects. They are thin abstractions of men, dangling in universal space, obsessed by memories of the womb, yet too modern, too faithless to crawl back to its warmth through the medium of shallow and decaying religions.[1]

Neider is not strictly correct in characterising all three protagonists as "not men of action." K.'s actions may be fruitless, but they are actions nevertheless. He is not the passive masochist of the two earlier novels: he may not have come to terms with his world, but he is aware of the necessity to do so in order to survive, and he constantly attempts to act upon his surroundings.

Neider sees *America* as a work of escape: escape from the sterile Europe of the years before World War I, escape from urgent personal problems by projecting them onto an entirely different background. America, the escapist paradise as seen by the Old World. It should, of course, be kept in mind that *America* is a comparatively immature work. The young Kafka was flexing his muscles, trying out his gift at greater length than in the even earlier pieces. It was not until *The Trial* that he realised he must stay with the inner dream world he had almost invented. After *America*, he no longer projected himself upon an alien external landscape, he brought the landscape inside, sought the desert within. But Neider is right to draw attention to the difference in approach between *America* and *The Trial*. In the latter novel, according to Neider, Kafka makes his most sustained attempt to deal with the father-fixation which so bedevilled his life.

The father is now seen as the group-father, the philistine, the man of night, of tenements, sewers, prejudice, superstition. *The Trial* is sex in stasis, sex recoiling on itself; it is sexual terror and inability to compromise, to share oneself.[2]

[1] Neider, p. 88.   [2] Neider, pp. 90-91.

And Neider draws attention to the development in style, now both more plastic and more visionary than in *America*. His description of *The Castle* is unusual. He interprets it as a less nightmarish, more relaxed work, abundant in domestic and fertility symbols. The air, it seems to him, is more open, the drama less acute. *The Castle*, he concludes, is a study of the dilemma of marriage.

This is a perfectly feasible, though unnecessarily limiting, argument to pursue. The Castle may well be irresponsible bachelorhood and the village responsible domesticity. But Kafka's symbols strike deeper than this, beyond the domestic to the racial, beyond the racial to the universal. Nevertheless, to this point one has been able to follow Neider sympathetically without necessarily being in wholehearted agreement with him. But the second half of his book, *Kafka: his Mind and Art*, sets out to expose the "secret meanings" of the novels. Devoting most of his space to *The Castle*, Neider attempts to prove that it "contains a cohesive and deliberate pattern of symbols and a cryptic meaning whose existence is indubitable and that it is no longer permissible to argue vaguely concerning its meaning."[3] He claims to have discovered four important facts about *The Castle*: that it consists of a vast network of sexual symbols; that it presents creatively the findings of psychoanalysis regarding states of consciousness; that it offers in detail the dynamics of the Oedipus complex; and that it contains a "web of nomenclatural symbolism."[4]

In general terms, Neider's argument appears reasonable and persuasive. It is, after all, not surprising, given his time, place and race, that Kafka should have come under the influence of Freud. He is Freudian only in the sense that we, having been born into a world still influenced by the fact of Christ, are all Christians. But Neider's detailed list of male and female sexual symbols

[3] Neider, p. 122.   [4] Neider, p. 122.

is exhausting and finally self-defeating. Windows, doors, churches are female symbols; planks, sticks, telephones are male. Even a man with his mouth hanging open is classified as a female symbol. If every concrete noun is to be accused of taking sides in the sex war, then it is possible to prove anything, or to prove nothing. More fruitful to pursue is Neider's theory of the states of consciousness, though even here it is important not to surrender so completely as to commit oneself to this and no other as the key to *The Castle*. It must always be remembered that the work of art is other than and more than any one explanation of it.

As a piece of Kafka criticism, Herbert Tauber's *Franz Kafka, eine Deutung seiner Werke*[5] is useful mainly in so far as it corrects Max Brod's healthily religious view of his friend. A more complex personality than Brod, Tauber is aware of the dangers of too directly relating art to life, literature to its sources; but in his eagerness to free Kafka from the almost purely biographical clutches of Brod, he is inclined to fall into the other trap of expecting the work of art to reveal, when examined, a perfectly functioning philosophical system. He is, nevertheless, admirable on Kafka's literary style:

> His originality of language derives from a passionate devotion to something struggling for expression, which rejects all exaggerated forms of, for example, philosophical nature, as being too imprecise. Kafka's words always appear as if veiled by a protective cloak, a garment woven out of his special experience. His similes are not only full of meaning, but—and this has been sensed by many who have turned all too light-heartedly to the task of interpreting Kafka's work—full of reservations. Kafka is entirely an introvert, representing faithfully the phenomena of his inner world, scorn-

[5] Translated as *Franz Kafka, an Interpretation of his Works* (London 1948).

ing contemporary modes of expression, because nothing but the most peculiarly personal language can, without falsifying it, bear true witness to the deepest depths. The apparent difficulty of some of his writings is not due to any artistic whim on his part. Rather is it the alleged obscurity and the outlandishness of his symbolic language which enable him, however paradoxical this may sound, to achieve his own undistorted clarity. So from its very inception his writing is preserved from the purple passage, from the hackneyed or the ambiguous expression. To search for the exact word is one of his passions. This may lead sometimes to wearisome, pedantically detailed discussions, but never to the commonplace and therefore well worn generality.[6]

Tauber's treatise, when it appeared in 1941, was the first to consider Kafka in any real detail. Scorning earlier generalisations, Tauber turned his attention to each of the works in turn, and this in itself was a useful and valuable task. His book is an admirably honest guide to Kafka. Like most commentators, Tauber considers *The Castle* to be Kafka's most comprehensive work; he views it as a kind of clarification of the forces that dominated Kafka's life:

The emotional background of the novel is provided by a fear of life, sensed continually as being in an imperfect and threatened position, after the experience that the plan of its life is one incessant, desperate battle, poised on the very brink of revolt, and yet, in its impotence, still striving with perpetual hope towards the future. The foreign, repellent figures of the villagers, the antipathy of the Landlady that increases to nervous hatred, the impertinence of the lower-grade clerks, betray the over-sensitive soft spots in a soul that labours under the burden of earthly things,

[6] Tauber, op. cit., p. xii.

while its longing for the higher has led it into constant conflict and struggle.[7]

Though to a much lesser extent than Brod, Tauber too is inclined to look for mystical, quasi-religious meanings in the works, and to a certain degree to neglect their more valid existence as works of art. Curiously, in many ways Tauber is the reverse side of the Brod coin, and there are times when one feels that his insistence on Kafka's "Unfruitfulness" is as unhelpful as Brod's concern with finding positive elements in his author.

Albert Camus, in his essay "Hope and Absurdity"[8] brings his formidably lucid intelligence to bear on the novels. Admittedly he has an almost Germanic concern with extra-aesthetic significance, though it differs from the Germanic approach in that it does at least recognise the existence of the work of art in and for itself. Still, Camus does attempt to squeeze philosophical juice out of what is a perfectly good aesthetic orange. He approaches Kafka's symbols as one would a sleeping but potentially dangerous dog:

A symbol is always in the realm of the general, and, however exact its translation, an artist can only restore movement to it: there is no word-for-word correspondence. Besides, nothing is more difficult to understand than a symbolic work. A symbol always goes beyond him who would use it and makes him say in fact more than he is conscious of expressing. In this respect, the surest means of laying hold of it is not to provoke it, to take up the work in no deliberate spirit, and not to look for its secret currents. For Kafka, in particular, it is fair to consent to his game, to approach the drama by its appearance and the novel by its form.[9]

[7] Tauber, op. cit., p. 132.
[8] In *The Kafka Problem* (ed. Flores).
[9] *The Kafka Problem*, p. 251.

When Camus talks of Kafka's naturalism, he makes it clear that he is referring not to events which seem natural to the reader, but to a state of affairs in which everything is accepted as natural by the character to whom they occur. This, however, is not natural, but dream-like. But there is no room in Camus's philosophy for the dream. The nightmare to him is the natural world, and Kafka's refusal to despair even at his inability to despair is what makes Camus categorise him as one of the first of the absurdists. At least this is a valid interpretation of Camus who was writing at a time before the theatre of the absurd had become a really strong force. Mirroring Kafka's brave admonition to himself about despair, Camus says "He will never be astonished enough at his own lack of astonishment."[10] This, to Camus, smacks of the absurd, whereas it can just as easily be understood as disillusion. Camus sees *The Castle* as the adventure of a soul in search of grace. Perhaps he is too lucid to properly comprehend Kafka's artistic ambiguity. *The Trial*, he considers, poses a problem which is to a certain extent solved by *The Castle*. But surely the problems posed are different ones: that they often co-exist is hardly relevant. K. and Joseph K. would gladly have exchanged their burdens.

Camus does, however, clearly understand that Kafka seeks not what is universal but what is true, and that it is possible that the two do not coincide.

An interesting contribution to Kafka studies was made fairly recently by Mark Spilka in *Dickens and Kafka*.[11] As its title implies, Mr Spilka's book is an examination of what he sees as the essential similarity of Dickens and Kafka, and he is helped in this by Kafka's admission of his enthusiasm for Dickens. In the course of his investigation of their affinity, Spilka offers a number of extremely perceptive insights into the artistic character and method

[10] *The Kafka Problem*, p. 252.
[11] Mark Spilka: *Dickens and Kafka* (London 1963).

of Kafka. Kafka, who was quite well-read in Dickens, did refer to *America* as his Dickens novel. But Spilka sees the principal connexion between the two authors in their common theme of the conflict between self and family, and, more particularly, between family and society. Other Kafka critics, including Vašata, Tedlock and Pascal have discussed the relationship between *David Copperfield* and *America*, often finding a meeting point in the grotesque element which was common to both novelists. But Spilka maintains that the similarities are deeper in origin, and more far-reaching. The incident, which we know of from the *Letter to my Father*, when the child Franz was locked out on the balcony in the middle of the night by his father is equated by Spilka with David Copperfield's five days of confinement:

This was [Kafka's] earliest memory of abuse; it accounts amply for his interest in David's brief ordeal, which he reshaped in *The Metamorphosis* to suit his needs, and which he repeated in *America* in more personal terms. The incident meant much to Kafka; though "only a small beginning," it seemed to crystal-lise that "sense of nothingness" within the home which characterised his childhood. Because of that isolation, imposed by a father who was clearly in-sensitive to the emotional needs of his own children, Kafka could sympathise with Dickens' personal suffering; and beyond this, he could identify with the writer's need to return to the scene of early "crimes" and set them right in his mind. For the fact remains, the most popular English novelist of the nineteenth century, the inventor (almost) of Christmas cheer and the warm family hearth, was as obsessed and tormented as Kafka by his boyhood troubles; as with Kafka, they reduced him in his dreams to an infantile state; and like Kafka, he repeated them again and again in his writings, to the point where the child's view of the

universe became the characteristic view in all his
novels, no different in its affective quality from the
author's own perspective.[12]

The Dickens influence is more strongly seen in Kafka's
themes than in his style or method. The willing slave-
labour for father-figures, expulsion from the womb of the
family, failure in heterosexual relationships, these can
be found in the older novelist. What Kafka has done is
to turn the physical suffering of Dickens into psychological torment. In the final analysis, this frees him from
Dickens' more excessively sentimental moments. It also
leads the creative tension onto a different, an inner
plane. As Spilka remarks, Kafka's quarrel with God
may be merely a higher stage of Dickens' quarrel with
society.

Kafka, however, had his own quarrel with society.
Rudolf Vašata,[13] who wrote about the Dickens-Kafka
influence well before Spilka, refutes both religion and
psychoanalysis. His orthodox Marxian viewpoint is not
really able to comprehend the complete Kafka. Dickens
is praised because he lived in a period of important social
and economic change. Kafka is unfortunate in that his
creative period concides with the decline and fall of the
Austro-Hungarian monarchy. Curiously, after years of
almost total rejection, Kafka is beginning to be seriously
considered by Soviet Russian critics. It is understandable,
if unfortunate, that Dmitri Zatonsky should concentrate
on the man in his milieu, the dissolving Habsburg world
again, and make the best he can of what he calls Kafka's
progressive social and political standpoint, but he is
reasonably acute about the author's spiritual isolation as
well: "Everywhere Kafka was alien, superfluous; the
general process of capitalist "alienation" was com-
pounded of "alienation" in private life. He felt himself

[12] Spilka, op. cit., pp. 40-41.
[13] In *The Kafka Problem* (ed. Flores).

a man without a country, without a people."[14] And Zatonsky is aware that Kafka does not so much describe as embody "a sickness of our time." But Kafka's pessimism is too much for him, and the despondency of the later works is piously deplored.

The point of view put forward by another Soviet critic, Boris Suchov[15] is somewhat more individual and considered. For Suchov, Kafka stands at the source of modern art; and, although his morbidity renders him incapable of perceiving the social forces that influence mankind, he is a great artist who managed to make his way beyond Expressionism. Suchov has to call Kafka decadent, but is obviously fascinated by so productive a decadence. For the most part, other Soviet critics who have written on Kafka follow variants of these lines. Their attitude is summed up by Tamara Motyleva[16] who considers that Kafka together with Proust and Joyce "expressed a certain philosophy whose foundations are very familiar to us from many old works of Russian decadence: the inscrutability of the world, the omnipotence of evil, the insurmountable solitude of man."

And so Kafka's deceptive simplicity continues to confound his critics. He is a realist, an absurdist, a pessimist, an optimist, a satirist, a religious philosopher, a nihilist. He writes about Everyman, he writes only of himself. He has been appropriated by the mystics and the Marxists, he has been the play-thing of essayists in search of a subject. Charles Neider, who nevertheless has his own cabalistic axe to grind, considers that misinterpretation of Kafka is threefold: literary, critical and philosophical.

[14] Dmitri Zatonsky in "Kafka Without Retouching" (*Voprosi Literaturi*, no. 5, 1964).

[15] Boris Suchov in "Kafka, His Life and Work" (*Znamya*, nos. 10-11, 1964).

[16] Tamara Motyleva (in *Novy Mir*, no. 11, 1963)

The entire Kafka controversy has existed under incredibly turbulent conditions, with both sides occasionally wandering into enemy territory and, through sheer ignorance or confusion, sniping at their own positions. In the main the supernaturalists have come out best under such conditions, not because of superior logic but because, based on turmoil and the vague, the unempirical, they have fought the battle on their own ground; besides, and more important, they have in a sense laid down the rules of the game, with their "inside" knowledge as divulged by Kafka's intimates and disciples, their exegeses in terms of absolutes, divine, original sin and all the rest of the mystical baggage. And the naturalist critics, failing to recognise the philosophical issues and the moral consequences involved, lulled by the belief that the controversy was only "literary" and therefore sealed from the realm of ethics, fascinated by the fantastic logic of the mystics and lured by the "key," supinely accepting reports from the disciples as gospel, even when at variance with their own reasoning and the evidence in the works of Kafka, and even adapting some of the impedimenta of the supernaturalists, have failed to fix their sights and consequently have fired mightily but in vain.[17]

Largely agreeing with this, one can conclude only by reiterating as concisely as possible one's own thoughts about this most disturbing of modern novelists: thoughts on his form, his subject-matter, and his meaning.

Kafka's form springs less from any literary forbear than from an acquaintance with Freudian psychoanalysis. His influence is his own dream-life. Whatever sense one can read into the stories and novels, their formal sense is that of the dream. Consequently, it is no doubt true that

---

[17] *The Kafka Problem* (ed. Flores), p. 402. (The same passage can be found, in slightly different form, in Neider's *Kafka, His Mind and Art.*)

the novels are full of symbols, but perhaps not as childishly or as directly as Neider would have us suppose. The truth of the dream is not unlike, is certainly not opposed to, the artist's truth. If there is a truth of the morning and a truth of the evening, then Kafka's is that of the evening, of the night, and of raw perception. His characters are not somnambulists, but they possess the somnambulist's ability to by-pass nature's waking laws. The law they all succumb to is dark and eternal, but not natural. Kafka, the seeker after truth, knew instinctively where to seek it, and therefore how to create it: in and through the dream. But dream is not the content which divides, it is the form which unites. Not since the perfect lyrics of Goethe have truth and form merged so fruitfully as in the work of this intellectual dreamer.

Kafka's subject is an integral part of his form, but one could call it the search for identity, the voyage of self-discovery, the quest for truth, bitterness at the transience and futility of life. To put it differently, it is the subject matter of all great novelists however variously approached. "Why do we live?" may well be a futile question, just as "How shall we fill in the time until we die?" is a frivolous one. But Kafka answers the frivolous question as well as the futile one. We shall fill in our time by our continual attempts at definition of ourselves. And once we have revealed ourselves, we can safely die.

Finally, what does it all mean? Does it really matter whether we view Kafka as religious philosopher manqué or as mad genius? He is certainly to be regarded not as a preacher but as an artist: an artist who can be understood in psychological terms without being completely limited by them. It surely must be admitted that the basis of Kafka's creativity is rooted in psychopathology. But whether the artist creates from sickness as Kafka did, or from health as Thomas Mann appeared to, the art that results is not to be understood purely as symptom. A rose, as Gertrude Stein might have said, is not the ground in which it was planted. Nor is *The Castle* a Freudian casebook. Whether or not Kafka benefited therapeutically from his art, he brought into being a vivid and meaningful world in three novels and a number of shorter pieces. By giving aesthetic shape to his pessimistic fears he dispelled them, and created from their shadows some of the most obsessively fascinating literary works of our century.

SELECT BIBLIOGRAPHY

I. BOOKS BY KAFKA

1. In German

(*a*) Original German Publications

Betrachtung (1913) Ernst Rowohlt, Leipzig.
Der Heizer, Ein Fragment (1913) Kurt Wolff, Leipzig.
Ein Hungerkünstler (1914) Verlag Die Schmiede, Berlin.
Die Verwandlung (1916) Kurt Wolff, Leipzig.
Das Urteil (1916) Kurt Wolff, Leipzig.
Ein Landarzt (1919) Kurt Wolff, Leipzig.
In Der Strafkolonie (1919) Kurt Wolff, Munich.
Der Prozess (1925) Verlag Die Schmiede, Berlin.
Das Schloss (1926) Kurt Wolff, Munich.
Amerika (1927) Kurt Wolff, Munich.
Beim Bau Der Chinesischen Mauer (1931) Gustav Kiepenheuer, Berlin.
Vor Dem Gesetz (1934) Schocken Verlag, Berlin.
Gesammelte Schriften (1935) Schocken Verlag, Berlin (Vols. I-IV);
    (1936) Verlag Henrich Mercy Sohn, Prague (Vol. v); (1937)
    Verlag Henrich Mercy Sohn, Prague. (Vol. vi)

(*b*) Other Editions

Gesammelte Schriften, edited by Max Brod, second edition (Schocken
    Books Inc. New York/Frankfurt am Main): *Der Prozess* (1950);
    Das Schloss (1951); *Tagebücher 1910-1923* (1951); *Briefe an
    Milena* ed. Willy Haas (1952); *Erzählungen* (1952); *Amerika*
    (1953); *Hochzeitsvorbereitungen auf dem Lande* (1953); *Beschreibung
    eines Kampfes* (1954,); *Briefe 1902-1924* (1958).

2. In English

Definitive edition published by Secker and Warburg:
The Castle, tr. Edwin and Willa Muir (1930).
The Trial, tr. Edwin and Willa Muir (1937).
America, tr. Willa and Edwin Muir (1938).
The Diaries Vol. 1 tr. Joseph Kresh (1948).
            Vol. 2 tr. Martin Greenberg and Hannah Arendt (1949).
In the Penal Settlement, tr. Willa and Edwin Muir (1949).
Letters to Milena, tr. James and Tania Stern (1953).

Wedding Preparations in the Country, tr. Ernst Kaiser and Eithne Wilkins
(1954).
Description of a Struggle and *The Great Wall of China*, tr. Willa and
Edwin Muir and James and Tania Stern (1960).

II. BOOKS ABOUT KAFKA

ANDERS, GÜNTHER. *Kafka*. Munich 1951. Translated as *Franz Kafka*.
London (Bowes and Bowes) 1960.
BEISSNER, FRIEDRICH. *Der Erzähler Franz Kafka*. Stuttgart 1952.
BROD, MAX. *Franz Kafka, eine Biographie*. Prague 1957. Translated as
Franz Kafka, a Biography. London (Secker and Warburg) 1947.
EISNER, PAVEL. *Franz Kafka and Prague*, New York (Arts) 1950.
FLORES, ANGEL (ed.). *The Kafka Problem*. New York 1946.
FLORES, ANGEL and HOMER SWANDEN (edd.). *Franz Kafka Today*.
New York 1958.
GOODMAN, PAUL. *Kafka's Prayer*. New York (Vanguard) 1947.
JANOUCH, GUSTAV. *Conversations with Kafka*. New York (Praeger) 1953.
NEIDER, CHARLES. *Kafka: his Mind and Art*. London (O.U.P.) 1949.
SPILKA, MARK. *Dickens and Kafka*. London (Dobson) 1963.
TAUBER, HERBERT. *Franz Kafka, eine Deutung seiner Werke*. Zurich
1941. Translated as *Franz Kafka, an Interpretation of his Work*.
London (Secker and Warburg) 1948.
UYTTERSPROT, HERMAN. *Praags Cachet*. Antwerp 1963.
WAGENBACH, KLAUS. *Franz Kafka: Eine Biographie seiner Jugend*. Bern
1958.
WELTSCH, FELIX. *Religion und Humor in Leben und Werk Franz Kafkas*
Berlin 1957.
WEST, REBECCA. *The Court and the Castle*. New Haven (Yale U.P.)
1957.